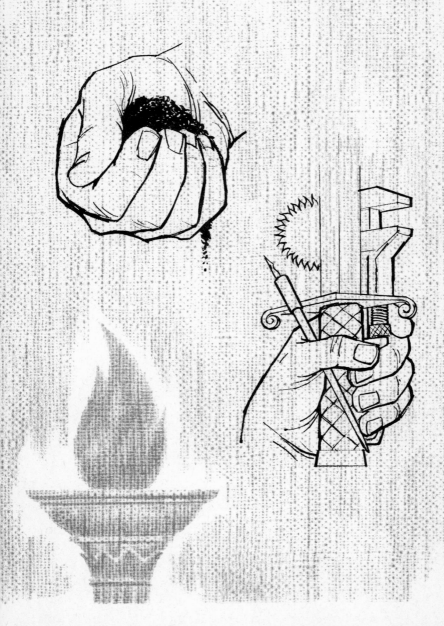

Bea

from Al and Mary Lou

WORDS THAT INSPIRE

A Treasury of

GREAT AMERICAN QUOTATIONS

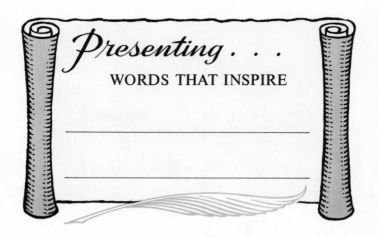

Presenting . . .

WORDS THAT INSPIRE

_____

_____

Great

American

Quotations

from

song and speech

poetry and prose

tracts and treatises

by our country's

great

men and women

*The wisdom of nations lies in
their proverbs which are brief
and pithy.*   WILLIAM PENN

WORDS THAT INSPIRE

A Treasury of

GREAT AMERICAN QUOTATIONS

*OUR COUNTRY'S LIFE & HISTORY
IN THE THOUGHTS OF ITS
MEN AND WOMEN*

☆

BY CHARLES HURD

SPECIAL ILLUSTRATED EDITION

J. G. FERGUSON PUBLISHING CO.
6 North Michigan Avenue
Chicago, Illinois

Oxford Bound in Leather and Fibre by Brown and Bigelow,
Saint Paul, Minnesota • A Division of Standard Packaging Corp.

First edition, *April, 1964*

WORDS THAT INSPIRE is a special illustrated edition of A TREASURY OF GREAT AMERICAN QUOTATIONS

ACKNOWLEDGMENTS

Sincere thanks are extended to the many publishers and individuals for permission to include material in this work. Every effort has been made to assign proper credits. If these have been omitted where they are due, they will be included in subsequent editions. Our grateful acknowledgment to:

Mrs. Rosemary Carr Benét for lines from the *Selected Works of Stephen Vincent Benét* published by Rinehart & Company, Inc. Copyright 1927 by Stephen Vincent Benét. Copyright renewed 1955 by Rosemary Carr Benét.

The Chicago *Tribune* for selections from the column conducted by the late Bert Leston Taylor.

Doubleday & Co., Inc., for lines from *Joyce Kilmer: Poems, Essays and Letters,* Volume One, by Joyce Kilmer. Copyright 1914, 1917, 1918 by Doubleday & Co., Inc. Reprinted by permission of the publisher; for lines from archy and mehitabel, by Don Marquis. Copyright 1927 by Doubleday & Co., Inc. Reprinted by permission of the publisher; for lines from *Dreams and Dust,* by Don Marquis. Copyright 1915 by Harper & Brothers. Reprinted by permission of Doubleday & Co., Inc.

Mrs. Norma Millay Ellis for lines from "The Philosopher," "Feast," "First Fig," "The Goose Girl," and "Travel," from *Collected Poems* by Edna St. Vincent Millay, published by Harper and Row, Publishers, Inc. Copyright 1921, 1922, 1923, 1948, 1950, 1951, by Edna St. Vincent Millay and Norma Millay Ellis. Reprinted by special permission of Mrs. Ellis.

Harcourt, Brace & World, Inc. for selections from "Primer Lesson" in *Slabs of the Sunburnt West,* by Carl Sandburg. Copyright 1922 by Harcourt, Brace & World, Inc.; renewed 1950 by Carl Sandburg. Reprinted by permission of the publishers; "Prayer" by Louis Untermeyer, Copyright 1914, by Harcourt, Brace & World, Inc.; renewed 1942 by Louis Untermeyer. Reprinted from his volume *Long Feud* by permission of the publishers; "Prayer for This House" from *This Singing World* edited by Louis Untermeyer, copyright, 1923, by Harcourt, Brace & World, Inc.; renewed, 1951, by Louis Untermeyer. Reprinted by permission of the publishers.

Harper & Row, Publishers, Inc., for selections from *Fables in Slang,* by George Ade; fragment from the poem "The Wanderer" in *The Hills Grow Smaller,* by Zoë Akins. Copyright 1937 by Zoë Akins Rumbold. Reprinted with the permission of Harper & Row, Publishers; lines from "Critic" from *The Lady Is Cold,* by E. B. White. Copyright 1929 by Harper & Brothers, renewed 1957 by E. B. White. Originally appeared in *The New Yorker,* and reprinted with the permission of Harper & Row, Publishers.

FOREWORD

THE editor and his publisher share a pardonable pride in this work devoted to the memorable quotations of Americans.

To introduce the quotations and make them more meaningful we have added a brief biography identifying the author and, where it is pertinent, the reason that made his words live.

Our country is rich in oratory, sermons, songs, literature, poems and statecraft—far too rich for a rounded inclusion in other excellent books of quotations that take the whole world and all of history as their sources. Even in this volume there is no room for the ephemeral wisecrack or the transient bright saying. Neither have these pages been burdened with long and often dull passages from works simply because their authors have achieved a certain fame.

This is a compilation of the pithy statements, homely phrases and bits of poetry that voice the progress of America and her way of life. While it stands alone, it is also a companion to the prior volumes, *A Treasury of Great American Speeches* and *A Treasury of Great American Letters*.

For the general reader we sincerely hope that this volume will represent a sharing of our heritage, and perhaps a guide line to broader reading in fields where quotations serve as reminders of possibly forgotten delights. For the student it may serve as a guide into new fields of exploration.

Two listings of the quotations are included to facilitate these purposes:

1. The Table of Contents lists the sources chronologically with key words to the content of the prose quotations. Titles are given for excerpts from poetry, songs and verses. Each quotation is numbered for easy reference. Sources are not listed for many prose quotations that have become proverbial; however, those referring to significant speeches, books and dates are included.

2. An alphabetical list of all the authors, their dates and professions is the Appendix.

No work of this kind can be "original." The author makes grateful acknowledgment to the gleaning done by many other anthologists in broader fields. But many quotations in this book are not to be found in others; they reflect the years of research expended on the editor's earlier "treasuries."

It is understood full well that each reader may find some favorite quotation omitted, and at the same time question the inclusion of others. In such cases, suggestions for revision in later editions will be welcomed.

Finally, gratitude must be expressed to the hundreds of gifted Americans, living and dead, whose minds and hearts have found expression for our inspiration and guidance in these quoted words.

CHARLES HURD

CONTENTS

III. BROADENING HORIZONS

FOUNDATIONS

JOHN WINTHROP (1588–1649)

CAMBRIDGE-EDUCATED and a successful young lawyer in London, Winthrop, a Puritan, emigrated to Massachusetts Bay Colony in 1630 and was elected governor for twelve terms. Immediately prior to his death he published a History of New England from 1630 to 1649. In 1645, when defending his governorship, he told the Magistrates:

. . . Liberty is the proper end and object of authority, and cannot subsist without it; and it is a liberty to that only which is good, just, and honest.

THE FIRST THANKSGIVING PROCLAMATION (June 20, 1676)

ON June 20, 1676 the governing council of Charlestown, Massachusetts, held a meeting to determine how best to express thanks for the good fortune that had seen their community securely established. By unanimous vote they instructed Edward Rawson, the clerk, to proclaim June 29 as a day of thanksgiving, our first.

The Holy God having by a long and Continual Series of his Afflictive dispensations in and by the present Warr with the Heathen Natives of this land, written and brought to pass bitter things against his own Covenant people in this wilderness, yet so that we evidently discern that in the midst of his judgements he hath remembered mercy, having remembered his Footstool in the day of his sore displeasure against us for our sins, with many singular Intimations of his Fatherly Compassion, and regard; reserving many of our Towns from Desolation Threatened, and attempted by the Enemy, and giving us especially of late with many of our Confederates many signal Advantages against them, without such Disadvantage to ourselves as formerly we have been sensible of, if it be the Lord's mercy that we are not consumed, It certainly bespeaks our positive Thankfulness, when our Enemies are in any

37

measure disappointed or destroyed; and fearing the Lord should take notice under so many Intimations of his returning mercy, we should be found an Insensible people, as not standing before Him with Thanksgiving, as well as lading him with our Complaints in the time of pressing Afflictions:

The Council has thought meet to appoint and set apart the 29th day of this instant June, as a day of Solemn Thanksgiving and praise to God for such his Goodness and Favour, many Particulars of which mercy might be Instanced, but we doubt not those who are sensible of God's Afflictions, have been as diligent to espy him returning to us; and that the Lord may behold us as a People offering Praise and thereby glorifying Him; the Council doth commend it to the Respective Ministers, Elders and people of this Jurisdiction; Solemnly and seriously to keep the same Beseeching that being perswaded by the mercies of God we may all, even this whole people offer up our bodies and souls as a living and acceptable Service unto God by Jesus Christ.

WILLIAM PENN (1644–1718)

THE founder of Pennsylvania joined the Society of Friends as an adult, at the cost of antagonizing his father, a knighted British admiral. Later he was granted a tract of land (now Pennsylvania) for his holy experiment in religious and political freedom, as repayment of a debt the crown owed his father. A student of Oxford, lawyer, philosopher and respected businessman in England, Penn was a devoted father to his colonists and his children alike. He expressed his teachings in his writings, especially in his two volumes of the *Fruits of Solitude* (1693) and *Advice to His Children* (1699).

1. The wisdom of nations lies in their proverbs, which are brief and pithy.

2. All excess is ill, but drunkeness if of the worst sort. It spoils health, dismounts the mind, and unmans men. It reveals secrets, is quarrelsome, lascivious, impudent, dangerous and bad.

3. Truth often suffers more by the heat of its defenders, than from the arguments of its opposers.

4. Men are generally more careful of the breed of their horses and dogs than of their children.

5. It were endless to dispute upon everything that is disputable.

6. Have a care where there is more sail than ballast.

7. Passion is a sort of fever of the mind, which ever leaves us weaker than it found us.

8. The public must and will be served.

9. . . . Much reading is an oppression of the mind, and extinguishes the natural candle, which is the reason of so many senseless scholars in the world.

10. It were better to be of no church, than to be bitter for any.

11. He that does good for good's sake seeks neither praise nor reward, though sure of both at the last.

12. Next to God, thy parents.

13. To be furious in religion is to be irreligiously religious.

14. To be like Christ is to be a Christian.   *His last words*

JONATHAN EDWARDS (1703–1758)

KNOWN as the "last of the great New England Calvinists," Edwards, by his mid-twenties had, by his forceful preaching already established himself as an imposing figure. Prior to that time he had been graduated from Yale at seventeen and had taught there. His sermons were fiery, notably "Sinners in the Hand of an Angry God." But today his precepts are recalled as those of an inspired man.

1. The material universe exists only in the mind.

2. *Resolved,* never to do anything which I should be afraid to do if it were the last hour of my life.   *Seventy Resolutions*

3. I assert that nothing ever comes to pass without a cause.

4. Intend to live in continual mortification, and never to expect or desire any worldly ease or pleasure.   *Diary, 1723*

5. This dictate of common sense.

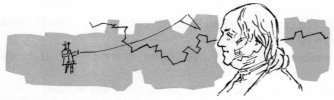

BENJAMIN FRANKLIN (1706–1790)

HIS long life helps to account for, but does not explain, the fantastic breadth of the genius of this man who could be described with equal accuracy as printer's apprentice, "Sage of the Revolution," a Doctor of Science who helped unmask Mesmer's claims, discoverer of the natural origin of electricity and one of the world's most prolific givers of good advice to the public. His works filled many volumes, principally *Poor Richard's Almanac* and his *Autobiography:* their contents—a wealth of proverbs and aphorisms seldom equalled.

1. At twenty years of age the will reigns; at thirty, the wit; and at forty, the judgement.

2. He that by the plow would thrive
   Himself must either hold or drive.

3. A Bible and a newspaper in every house, a good school in every district—all studied and appreciated as they merit—are the principal support of virtue, morality and civil liberty.

4. Carelessness does more harm than a want of knowledge.

5. For want of a nail, the shoe was lost; for want of a shoe the horse was lost; and for want of a horse the rider was lost, being overtaken and slain by the enemy, all for want of care about a horseshoe nail.

6. The Cat in Gloves catches no Mice.

7. Teach your child to hold his tongue,
   He'll learn fast enough to speak.

8. Little Boats should keep near Shore.

9. A good conscience is a continual Christmas.

10. Constant complaint is the poorest sort of pay for all the comforts we enjoy.

11. The great secret of succeeding in conversation is to admire little, hear much; always to distrust our own reason, and sometimes that of our friends; never to pretend to wit, but to make that of others appear as much as we possibly can; to hearken to what is said, and to answer to the purpose.

12. A man must have a good deal of vanity who believes, and a good deal of boldness who affirms, that all the doctrines he holds are true, and all he rejects are false.

13. Creditors have better memories than debtors. And creditors are a superstitious sect, great observers of set days and time.

14. He that riseth late must trot all day, and shall scarce overtake his business by night.

15. It is easier to suppress the first desire than to satisfy all that follow it.

16. Display is as false as it is costly.

17. Eat to please thyself, but dress to please others.

18. The early morning has gold in its mouth.

19. Early to bed and early to rise,
Makes a man healthy, wealthy, and wise.

20. If you know how to spend less than you get you have the philosopher's stone.

21. Beware of little expenses; a small leak will sink a great ship.

22. If a man empties his purse into his head, no one can take it from him.

23.   The body
                        of
              Benjamin Franklin Printer,
  (Like the cover of an old book, its contents torn out
      And stript of its lettering and gilding),
           Lies here, food for worms;
          But the work shall not be lost,
      For it will (as he believed) appear once more
                    In a new
And more elegant edition, revised and corrected by the Author.
                              Epitaph written in 1728

24. None preaches better than the ant, and she says nothing.

25. A cheerful face is nearly as good for an invalid as healthy weather.

26. If you would not be forgotten as soon as you are dead, either write things worth reading or do things worth writing.

27. Fools make feasts, and wise men eat them.

28. There are three faithful friends: an old wife, an old dog, and ready money.

29. Keep flax from fire, youth from gaming.

30. There was never yet a truly great man that was not at the same time truly virtuous.

31. Fraud and deceit are ever in a hurry. Take time for all things. Great haste makes great waste.

32. In humility imitate Jesus and Socrates.

33. Pity and forbearance should characterize all acts of justice.

34. Those who would give up essential liberty to purchase a little temporary safety deserve neither liberty nor safety.

35. Where liberty dwells, there is my country.

36. Were the offer made true, I would engage to run again, from beginning to end, the same career of life. All I would ask should be the privilege of the author, to correct, in a second edition, certain errors of the first.

37. Dost thou love life? Then do not squander time, for that is the stuff life is made of.

38. If you would be loved, love and be lovable.

39. A single man has not nearly the value he would have in a state of union. He is an incomplete animal. He resembles the odd half of a pair of scissors.

40. Where there's marriage without love, there will be love without marriage.

41. If you would know the value of money, go and try to borrow some.

42. Necessity knows no law.

43. Let thy child's first lesson be obedience, and the second will be what thou wilt.

44. Plough deep while sluggards sleep.

45. Even peace may be purchased at too high a price.

46. Pride that dines on vanity, sups on contempt.

47. Never leave that till to-morrow which you can do to-day.

48. He that blows the coals in quarrels he has nothing to do with has no right to complain if the sparks fly in his face.

49. If men are so wicked (as we see them now) with religion, what would they be if without it?

50. 'Tis more noble to forgive, and more manly to despise, than to revenge an Injury.

51. He that falls in love with himself will have no rivals.

52. Fatigue is the best pillow.

53. One to-day is worth two to-morrows.

54. We must indeed all hang together, or most assuredly we shall all hang separately.

At the signing of the Declaration of Independence

55. What maintains one vice would bring up two children.

56. There never was a good war or a bad peace.

Letter, 1773

57. If your riches are yours, why don't you take them with you to t'other world?

58. An undutiful Daughter will prove an unmanageable Wife.

59. Some are weather-wise, some are otherwise.

60. There's many witty men whose brains can't fill their bellies.

61. A ploughman on his legs is higher than a gentleman on his knees.

62. Handle your tools without mittens.

63. But in this world nothing is sure but death and taxes.

64. Reckless youth makes rueful age.

SAMUEL ADAMS (1722–1803)

HAD Samuel Adams been less a firebrand and more a politician, he might have achieved the presidency, won by his second cousin John; but this was not his character. Long before the Revolution he joined John Hancock in forming the Sons of Liberty and helped to organize the Boston Tea Party. He was most eloquent at the Continental Congress, but after Independence was declared his political influence declined. Conservatives later called him an "agitator."

1. Among the natural rights of the colonists are these: first, a right to *life;* secondly, a right to liberty; thirdly to property; together with the right to support and defend them in the best manner they can.

2. Our union is now complete; our constitution composed,

established and approved. You are now the guardians of your own liberties.

3. We have no other alternative than independence, or the most ignominious and appalling servitude. The legions of our enemies thicken on our plains; desolation and death mark their bloody career; whilst the mangled corpses of our countrymen seem to cry out to us as a Voice from Heaven.

GEORGE WASHINGTON (1732–1799)

IT would be presumptuous, even if possible, to give a thumbnail sketch of Washington; suffice it to record that he was equal to all the opportunities for leadership accorded him, and certainly not the prig pictured by Parson Weems. Washington actually wrote and spoke relatively little compared to many of his compatriots. These selections begin with his correspondence and end with the celebrated injunction against permanent foreign alliances from his Farewell Address.

1. A slender acquaintance with the world must convince every man that actions, not words, are the true criterion of the attachment of friends; and that the most liberal professions of good-will are very far from being the surest marks of it.

2. Few men have virtue to withstand the highest bidder.

3. I hope I shall always possess firmness and virtue enough to maintain what I consider the most enviable of all titles, the character of an "Honest Man."

4. Labour to keep alive in your breast that little spark of celestial fire,—conscience.

5. To persevere in one's duty and to be silent is the best answer to calumny.

6. Be courteous to all, but intimate with few; and let those few be well tried before you give them your confidence.

7. It [gambling] is the child of avarice, the brother of iniquity, and the father of mischief.

8. Let us raise a standard to which the wise and honest can repair; the event is in the hands of God.

9. Liberty, when it begins to take root, is a plant of rapid growth.

10. The foolish and wicked practice of profane cursing and swearing is a vice so mean and low that every person of sense and character detests and despises it.

11. In a free and republican government, you cannot restrain the voice of the multitude. Every man will speak as he thinks or, more properly, without thinking, and consequently will judge of effects without attending to their causes.

12. Associate with men of good quality, if you esteem your own reputation, for it is better to be alone than in bad company.

13. I never mean, unless some peculiar circumstance should compel me to do it, to possess another slave by purchase, it being among my first wishes to see some plan adopted by which slavery in this country may be abolished by law.

14. Arbitrary power is most easily established on the ruins of liberty abused to licentiousness.

15. To be prepared for war is the most effectual means of preserving peace.

16. Observe good faith and justice toward all nations.

17. 'Tis our true policy to steer clear of permanent alliances, with any portion of the foreign world—as far, I mean, as we are now at liberty to do it.

JOHN ADAMS (1735–1826)

THE second President was a distinguished debater, statesman, and ambassador, but seldom dramatically eloquent. Interestingly enough, his most enduring words were discovered in letters to his wife. The first two quotations below are from a letter to her written July 2, 1776, and the third from a later letter when he was President. In addition he left a poignant deathbed exclamation. Not knowing that Jefferson had died hours earlier, he said, "Thank God, Jefferson still lives!"

1. Yesterday the greatest question was decided which ever was debated in America; and a greater perhaps never was, nor

will be, decided among men. A resolution was passed without one dissenting colony, that these United Colonies are, and of right ought to be, free and independent States.

2. The die was now cast; I had passed the Rubicon. Swim or sink, live or die, survive or perish with my country was my unalterable determination.

3. Every man in it [the Congress] is a great man, an orator, a critic, a statesman; and therefore every man upon every question must show his oratory, his criticism, and his political abilities.

4. As the happiness of the people is the sole end of government, so the consent of the people is the only foundation of it, in reason, morality, and the natural fitness of things.

Proclamation, 1774

PATRICK HENRY (1736–1799)

THE contrary in character of Adams, Henry, a red-headed Virginia lawyer, though a leader among the "Radicals," failed to achieve great leadership among the Founding Fathers. However in a few inspired instances he bespoke the rousing fervor of revolution.

1. Tarquin and Caesar each had his Brutus, Charles the First his Cromwell, and George the Third *may profit by their example*. If *this* be treason, make the most of it.

Speech on the Stamp Act, May 28, 1765

2. I am not a Virginian, but an American.

Speech in First Continental Congress, 1774

3. I have but one lamp by which my feet are guided, and that is the lamp of experience.

.   .   .   .

I know of no way of judging of the future but by the past.

.   .   .   .

Is life so dear, or peace so sweet, as to be purchased at the price of chains and slavery? Forbid it, Almighty God! I know not what course others make take, but as for me, give me liberty, or give me death! *Speech in Virginia Convention, 1775*

JOHN HANCOCK (1737–1793)

FEW men had more material things to lose in the Revolution than John Hancock, wealthy Boston trader and shipowner. Yet he was to become president of the Continental Congress, and sign his name boldly on the Declaration of Independence. Seldom eloquent, he rose to unusual heights in addressing Bostonians after the Battle of Concord.

We fear not death. That gloomy night, that pale-faced moon, and the affrighted stars that hurried through the sky, can witness that we fear not death.

THOMAS PAINE (1737–1809)

THE English-born Paine deeply influenced thought in three countries by his writings. His "Crisis" pamphlets during the American Revolution inspired patriotism in America but attacks on systematized religion and George Washington caused his virtual ostracism. In Britain the publication of his work, *The Rights of Man,* endorsing the French Revolution, forced him to flee to France. There as a member of the Convention, he eventually landed in prison. But even so, his prose and poetry, including also *The Age of Reason* and *The Liberty Tree,* created for him a formidable posthumous reputation.

1. These are the times that try men's souls.

2. The nearer any disease approaches to a crisis, the nearer it is to a cure. [Danger and deliverance make their advances together; and it is only in the last push that one or the other takes the lead.]

3. Calumny is a vice of curious constitution; trying to kill it keeps it alive; leave it to itself and it will die a natural death.

4. What we obtain too cheap, we esteem too lightly;—'tis dearness only that gives everything its value.

5. Panics, in some cases, have their uses; they produce as much good as hurt. Their duration is always short; the mind soon grows through them and acquires a firmer habit than before.

6. Not a place upon earth might be so happy as America. Her situation is remote from all the wrangling world, and she has nothing to do but to trade with them.

7. Civilisation, or that which is so called, has operated two ways to make one part of society more affluent and the other part more wretched than would have been the lot of either in a natural state.

8. Tyranny, like hell, is not easily conquered; yet we have this consolation with us, that the harder the conflict the more glorious the triumph.

9. A thing moderately good is not so good as it ought to be. Moderation in temper is always a virtue; but moderation in principle is always a vice.

10. Whatever has a tendency to promote the civil intercourse of nations by an exchange of benefits is a subject as worthy of philosophy as of politics.

11. Human nature is not of itself vicious.

12. Virtue is not hereditary.

13. War involves in its progress such a train of unforeseen and unsupposed circumstances that no human wisdom can calculate the end. It has but one thing certain, and that is to increase taxes. *Prospects on the Rubicon, 1787*

14. The sublime and the ridiculous are often so nearly related, that it is difficult to class them separately. One step below the sublime, makes the ridiculous; and one step more above the ridiculous, makes the sublime again.

15. Man worships not himself, but his Maker; and the liberty of conscience which he claims is not for the service of himself, but of his God.

16. The world is my country, all mankind are my brethren, and to do good is my religion. I believe in one God and no more.

17. In a chariot of light from the region of day
    The Goddess of liberty came.
Ten thousand celestials directed the way
    And hither conducted the dame.
A fair budding branch from the gardens above,
    Where millions with millions agree,

> She brought in her hand as a pledge of her love,
>> And the plant she named Liberty Tree.

. . . .

> From the east to the west blew the trumpet to arms!
>> Through the land let the sound of it flee;
> Let the far and the near all unite, with a cheer,
>> In defence of our Liberty Tree.

The Liberty Tree

THOMAS JEFFERSON (1743–1826)

THE third President was but one of the "Virginia gentlemen" notable as statesmen, philosophers, agriculturists and lifelong students of all arts and sciences. This group, unprecedented in stature, was the product of a time unparalleled in our history. It was Jefferson who drafted the Declaration of Independence; he was to found the University of Virginia. First Washington's closest confidant, he later broke away to lead a liberal political party—the Republicans—from whom the Democratic Party now claims political descent. Now known for his eloquence in speaking, he wrote with force and clarity. His work shows greater moderation and breadth than Paine's, possibly because he enjoyed by background a greater social and economic security than the latter, the son of a corset maker.

1. When, in the course of human events, it becomes necessary for one people to dissolve the political bonds which have connected them with another, and to assume among the powers of the earth the separate and equal station to which the laws of nature and of nature's God entitle them, a decent respect to the opinions of mankind requires that they should declare the causes which impel them to separation.

. . . .

We hold these truths to be self-evident: that all men are created equal; that they are endowed by their Creator with certain inalienable rights; that among these are life, liberty, and the pursuit of happiness.

. . . .

. . . we mutually pledge to each other our lives, our fortunes, and our sacred honor.   *The Declaration of Independence*

2. Equal and exact justice to all men, of whatever state of persuasion, religious or political; peace, commerce and honest friendship with all nations—entangling alliances with none; the support of the State governments in all their rights, as the most competent administrations of our domestic concerns, and the surest bulwarks against anti-republican tendencies; the preservation of the general government in its whole constitutional vigor, as the sheet anchor of our peace at home and safety abroad; . . . freedom of religion; freedom of the press; freedom of person under the protection of the habeus corpus; and trial by juries impartially selected,—these principles form the bright constellation which has gone before us, and guided our steps through an age of revolution and reformation.   *First Inaugural Address, 1801*

3. Rebellion to tyrants is obedience to God.

Motto on his seal

4. A little rebellion now and then is a good thing, and as necessary in the political world as storms in the physical.

Letter, 1787

5. All authority belongs to the people.

6. Advertisements contain the only truths to be relied on in a newspaper.

7. Those who labor in the earth are the chosen people of God, if He ever had a chosen people, whose breasts He has made His peculiar deposit for substantial and genuine virtue.

8. Never put off till tomorrow what you can do today.

9. No knowledge can be more satisfactory to a man than that of his own frame, its parts, their functions and actions.

10. I am mortified to be told that, in the United States of America, the sale of a book can become a subject of inquiry, and of criminal inquiry, too.

11. The time to guard against corruption and tyranny is before they have gotten hold of us. It is better to keep the wolf out of the fold than to trust to drawing his teeth and talons after he shall have entered.

12. The habit of using ardent spirits by men in office has

occasioned more injury to the public, and more trouble to me, than all other causes. Were I to commence my administration again, the first question I would ask respecting a candidate for office would be, Does he use ardent spirits?

13. The happiest moments of my life have been the few which I have passed at home in the bosom of my family.

14. I am for freedom of religion and against all maneuvers to bring about a legal ascendancy of one sect over another.

15. France, freed from that monster, Bonaparte, must again become the most agreeable country on earth. It would be the second choice of all whose ties of family and fortune give a preference to some other one, and the first choice of all not under those ties.

16. The people are the only sure reliance for the preservation of our liberty.

17. The will of the people is the only legitimate foundation of any government, and to protect its free expression should be our first object.

18. The God who gave us life, gave us liberty at the same time.

19. If I could not go to heaven but with a party [political] I would not go at all.

20. When a man assumes a public trust, he should consider himself as public property.

21. If a due participation of office is a matter of right, how are vacancies to be obtained? Those by death are few; by resignation, none.

22. It is more dangerous that even a guilty person should be punished without the forms of law than that he should escape.

HENRY KNOX (1750–1806)

FEW remember Knox for his many distinctions as a trusted officer under Washington in the Revolution, first Secretary of War, and founder of the Society of Cincinnati. He is immortalized by a phrase in a letter to Washington March 19, 1787 which on publication gave a ringing title to our first President, who was indeed the father of his country.

Were an energetic and judicious system to be proposed with your signature it would be a circumstance highly honorable to your fame . . . and doubly entitle you to the glorious republican epithet, *The Father of your Country.*

NATHAN HALE (1755–1776)

THE young school teacher, recently commissioned in the Connecticut militia, was captured near what is now Grand Central Station in New York City, and hanged without trial as a spy. According to later reports from his captors, these were his last words:

I only regret that I have but one life to lose for my country.

HENRY (LIGHT-HORSE HARRY) LEE (1756–1818)

TO Knox's tribute, Colonel Lee, another distinguished officer and father of Robert E. Lee, added the capstone in the resolutions adopted by the Congress on the death of Washington in 1799.

A citizen first in war, first in peace, and first in the hearts of his countrymen.

ALEXANDER HAMILTON (1757–1804)

THE young student from the West Indies, who became Washington's aide-de-camp and later showed his financial genius as the first and youngest Secretary of the Treasury, eventually died in a duel with Aaron Burr. He yielded a powerful influence in the development of federal fiscal and political policies after the Revolution, particularly by his contribution to the *Federalist Papers.*

1. Constitutions should consist only of general provisions; the reason is that they must necessarily be permanent, and that

they cannot possibly calculate for the possible change of things.

2. A national debt, if it is not excessive, will be to us a national blessing.

3. Learn to think continentally.

TIMOTHY DWIGHT (1752–1817)

THE Revolutionary period did not yield only statesmen. Dr. Dwight, author and educator who died in office as President of Yale, was a notable preacher and teacher, often quoted.

The Bible is a window in this prison-world, through which we may look into eternity.

PHILIP FRENEAU (1752–1832)

AND poets won recognition too. Freneau, known as the "poet of the American Revolution," is remembered for his eulogy to Franklin.

But matchless Franklin! What a few
Can hope to rival such as you.
Who seized from kings their sceptred pride
And turned the lightning's darts aside.
On the Death of Benjamin Franklin

JOEL BARLOW (1754–1812)

BARLOW, dividing his time between diplomacy and poetry, set a precedent for American folk poetry. Few remember him as the U.S. consul to Algiers who secured the release of many American prisoners taken by the Barbary pirates, or that he died of exposure on a mission to Napoleon that caught him up in the retreat from Moscow. But we do find this memorial to his good humor.

For now, the corn house filled, the harvest home,
    Th' invited neighbors to the husking come;
A frolic scene, where work and mirth and play
    Unite their charms to cheer the hours away.

The Husking Bee

FLOWERING YEARS

JOHN MARSHALL (1755–1835)

THE fourth Chief Justice and holder of that office longer than any other man [1801–1835] largely guided the Supreme Court's interpretations of the Constitution into legal application.

The Government of the Union, then, is emphatically and truly a government of the people. In form and in substance it emanates from them. Its powers are granted by them, and are to be exercised directly on them and for their benefit.

Opinion: McCulloch vs. Maryland, 1819

JAMES MONROE (1758–1831)

THE fifth President is best known for promulgation of "The Monroe Doctrine" which he drew up with John Quincy Adams in 1823, a document called forth by many succeeding Presidents in times of crisis.

1. National honor is national property of the highest value.
First Inaugural Address, 1817
2. The American continents . . . are henceforth not to be considered as subjects for future colonization by any European powers.

. . . .

We owe it, therefore, to candor, and to the amicable relations existing between the United States and those powers to declare that we should consider any attempt on their part to extend their system to any portion of this hemisphere as dangerous to our peace and safety. With the existing colonies or dependencies of any European power we . . . shall not interfere. But with the governments . . . whose independence we have . . . acknowledged, we could not view any interposition for the purpose of oppressing them, or controlling, in any other manner, their destiny, by any European

57

power, in any other light than as a manifestation of an unfriendly disposition towards the United States.

The Monroe Doctrine, 1823

FISHER AMES (1758–1808)

FROM this Massachusetts statesman-orator, advice.

No man ever did or ever will become truly eloquent without being a constant reader of the Bible, and an admirer of the purity and sublimity of its language.

ST. JOHN HONEYWOOD (1763–1798)

SUCCESSFUL lawyers often have their careers obscured by their clients, but this amateur poet struck off a verse that still is quoted.

When Darby saw the setting sun
    He swung his scythe, and home he run,
Sat down, drank off his quart, and said,
    "My work is done, I'll go to bed."
"My work is done!" retorted Joan,
    "My work is done! Your constant tone,
But hapless woman ne'er can say,
    'My work is done' till judgment day."

Darby and Joan

JOHN QUINCY ADAMS (1767–1848)

THE sixth President, and son of the second, was both a diplomat and an inspirational speaker. Like his sophisticated New England colleagues, "Old Man Eloquent" was not embarrassed to break into verse.

1. Think of your forefathers! Think of your posterity!

Speech, Plymouth, 1802

2. Westward the star of empire takes its way.
3. "Man wants but little here below
     Nor wants that little long."
   'Tis not exactly with me so;
     But 'tis so in the song.
   My wants are many, and, if told,
     Would muster many a score;
   And were each wish a mint of gold,
     I still should long for more.   *The Wants of Man*

4. This is the last of earth! I am content.   *His last words*

DAVID EVERETT (1767–1813)

WHEN this New Hampshire law-yer, then only twenty-seven, sat down and wrote a "recitation" for a seven-year-old friend, Ephraim H. Farrar, he created an American proverb.

You'd scarce expect one of my age
To speak in public on the stage;
And if I chance to fall below
Demosthenes or Cicero,
Don't view me with a critic's eye,
But pass my imperfections by.
Large streams from little fountains flow,
Tall oaks from little acorns grow.

ANDREW JACKSON (1767–1845)

THE seventh President, formerly famous military leader and latterly politican-statesman, represented a dramatic blending of sentiment, patriotism, and practical politics, characterized by a stubborn will.

1. Our federal Union; it must be preserved.
   Toast on Jefferson's birthday anniversary, 1830

2. To the victors belong the spoils.

On political patronage after election

3. Peace, above all things, is to be desired, but blood must sometimes be spilled to obtain it on equable and lasting terms.

4. Heaven will be no heaven to me if I do not meet my wife there.

JOSEPH HOPKINSON (1770–1842)

A lawyer and judge of considerable note in his time, all else is generally forgotten about Hopkinson except an inspired poem he produced in 1798, for which hymn music later was composed.

Hail, Columbia! happy land!
Hail, ye heroes! heaven-born band!
    Who fought and bled in Freedom's cause,
    Who fought and bled in Freedom's cause,
And when the storm of war was gone,
Enjoyed the peace your valor won.
    Let independence be our boast,
    Ever mindful what it cost;
    Ever grateful for the prize,
    Let its altar reach the skies!

Hail, Columbia (first stanza)

HOSEA BALLOU (1771–1852)

THIS clergyman aroused considerable controversy as a foremost proponent of universalism. His sermons are noted for their seemingly unorthodox linking of religious expression to daily experience.

1. Disease is the retribution of outraged Nature.

2. Education commences at the mother's knee, and every

word spoken within the hearing of little children tends towards the formation of character.

3. Energy, like the Biblical grain of mustard seed will remove mountains.

4. Error is always more busy than truth.

5. Theories are always very thin and unsubstantial; experience only is tangible.

6. There is one inevitable criterion of judgment touching religious faith in doctrinal matters. Can you reduce it to practice? If not, have none of it.

7. Not the least misfortune in a prominent falsehood is the fact that tradition is apt to repeat it for truth.

8. Real happiness is cheap enough, yet how dearly we pay for its counterfeit.

9. Idleness is emptiness; the tree in which the sap is stagnant remains fruitless.

10. Moderation is the key of lasting enjoyment.

11. A religion which requires persecution to sustain it is of the devil's propagation.

12. Between the humble and the contrite heart and the majesty of heaven there are no barriers; the only password is prayer.

13. Pretension almost always overdoes the original, and hence exposes itself.

14. Most people who commit a sin count on some personal benefit therefrom, but profanity has not even this excuse.

15. True repentance always involves reform.

16. A chaste and lucid style is indicative of the same personal traits in the author.

17. Suspicion is far more apt to be wrong than right; oftener unjust than just. It is no friend to virtue, and always an enemy to happiness.

18. Has not God borne with you these many years? Be ye tolerant of others.

19. Falsehood is cowardice,—truth is courage.

20. Gratitude is the fairest blossom which springs from the soul; and the heart of man knoweth none more fragrant.

21. Hatred is self-punishment.

WILLIAM HENRY HARRISON (1773–1841)

THE ninth President served the shortest of all Presidential terms. Exhausted from a strenuous campaign, he died of pneumonia a month after his Inaugural, but his Inaugural Address included often-quoted statements of basic principles.

1. We admit of no government by divine right.

2. Never with my consent shall an officer of the people, compensated for his services out of their pockets, become the pliant instrument of the Executive will.

3. A decent and manly examination of the acts of Government should be not only tolerated, but encouraged.

4. The delicate duty of devising schemes of revenue should be left where the Constitution has placed it—with the immediate representatives of the people.

5. If parties in a republic are necessary to secure a degree of vigilance to keep the public functionaries within the bounds of law and duty, at that point their usefulness ends.

LYMAN BEECHER (1775–1863)

THE father of the eloquent Henry Ward Beecher and Harriet Beecher Stowe, a clergyman, believed a principle of public debate.

No great advance has ever been made in science, politics, or religion, without controversy.

HENRY CLAY (1777–1852)

THIS fiery man from the "West," spokesman for western expansion, sprinkled half a century of speeches in and out of Washington, with observations and precepts as applicable today as in his time.

1. There is no power like that of oratory. Caesar controlled men by exciting their fears, Cicero by captivating their affections and swaying their passions. The influence of the one perished with its author; that of the other continues to this day.

2. Political parties serve to keep each other in check, one keenly watching the other.

3. I have heard something said about allegiance to the South: I know no South, no North, no East, no West, to which I owe any allegiance.

4. Sir, I would rather be right than President.

5. Government is a trust, and the officers of the government are trustees; and both the trust and the trustees are created for the benefit of the people.

6. If you wish to avoid foreign collision, you had better abandon the ocean.

7. It would not be thought very just or wise to arraign the honorable professions of law and physic because the one produces the pettifogger and the other the quack.

8. I have doubtless committed many errors and indiscretions, over which you have thrown the broad mantle of charity. But I can say, and in the presence of my God and of this assembled multitude I do say, that I have honestly served my country—that I have never wronged it—and that, however unprepared I lament that I am to appear in the Divine Presence on other accounts, I invoke the justice of His judgment on my official conduct without the smallest apprehension of His displeasure.

9. The arts of power and its minions are the same in all countries and in all ages. It marks its victim; denounces it; and excites the public odium and the public hatred, to conceal its own abuses and encroachments.

LORENZO DOW (1777–1834)

AN evangelist, this eccentric preacher wrote a definition of Calvinism in a verse since used to describe many things.

> You can and you can't,
> You shall and you shan't;
> You will and you won't;
> You'll be damned if you do,
> And you'll be damned if you don't.

WASHINGTON ALLSTON (1779–1843)

A successful portrait painter, Allston also set down his observations in writing. One journal entry tells of the rewards of art.

The love of gain never made a painter but it has married many.

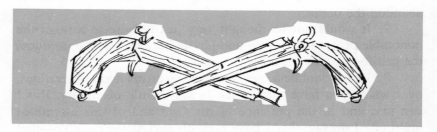

STEPHEN DECATUR (1779–1820)

DURING a brilliant naval career which brought him fame in battles in the Tripolitan War and the War of 1812, Decatur made an enemy of James Barron, a disgraced officer who, on March 22, 1820, mortally wounded him in a duel at Bladensburg, Maryland. But Decatur lives in a toast he propounded at a banquet in Norfolk in 1816.

Our country! In her intercourse with foreign nations, may she always be in the right; but our country, right or wrong.

FRANCIS SCOTT KEY (1779–1843)

ON the night of September 14, 1814, a British squadron in Chesapeake Bay shelled Fort McHenry. On board the flagship was a handful of civilians picked up and detained in order to preserve secrecy: one of these was a lawyer from Washington, Key. While he watched the bombardment, the lawyer penned an inspired lyric.

Oh, say can you see by the dawn's early light
    What so proudly we hailed at the twilight's last
        gleaming?
Whose broad stripes and bright stars, thro' the perilous
    fight,
    O'er the ramparts we watched were so gallantly
        streaming?
And the rockets' red glare, the bombs bursting in air,
    Gave proof thro' the night that our flag was still
        there.

      .   .   .   .

Oh, say, does that star-spangled banner yet wave,
O'er the land of the free and the home of the brave?

      .   .   .   .

Then conquer we must, for our cause it is just,—
    And this be our motto,—"In God is our trust!"
                   The Star-Spangled Banner

CLEMENT CLARKE MOORE
(1779–1863)

A famous educator and scholar, publisher of the first Hebrew and Greek lexicon issued in America. Dr. Moore also wrote poetry in his lighter moments—one beloved selection was first published in 1823.

'Twas the night before Christmas, when all through the
    house
    Not a creature was stirring,—not even a mouse:
The stockings were hung by the chimney with care,
    In hopes that St. Nicholas soon would be there.

      .   .   .   .

    As he drove out of sight
"Happy Christmas to all, and to all a good-night!"
                  A Visit from St. Nicholas

HORACE BINNEY (1780–1875)

A lawyer by profession, and a biographer by avocation, Binney in his writings showed much philosophical talent.

Nature is the most thrifty thing in the world; she never wastes anything; she undergoes change, but there's no annihilation, the essence remains—matter is eternal.

TIMOTHY FLINT (1780–1840)

AS an author and itinerant missionary, now noted primarily for his works on Daniel Boone, Flint was a sort of rural philosopher.

Next to temperance, a quiet conscience, a cheerful mind and active habits, I place early rising as a means of health and happiness.

WILLIAM ELLERY CHANNING (1780–1842)

A distinguished Harvard scholar and preacher, Channing, a Unitarian, exercised great liberalizing influence in religious thought and was credited with guiding the development of Emerson and Holmes.

1. One anecdote of a man is worth a volume of biography.
2. The sages and heroes of history are receding from us. . . . But time has no power over the name and deeds and words of Jesus Christ.
3. (On dancing) No amusement seems more to have a foundation in our nature. The animation of youth overflows spontaneously in harmonious movements. The true idea of dancing entitles

it to favor. Its end is to realize perfect grace in motion; and who does not know that a sense of the graceful is one of the highest faculties of our nature?

4. A man in earnest finds means, or, if he cannot find, creates them.

5. Mistake, error, is the discipline through which we advance.

6. Faith is love taking the form of aspiration.

7. Be true to your own highest convictions.

8. Every man is a volume, if you know how to read him.

9. Every mind was made for growth, for knowledge; and its nature is sinned against when it is doomed to ignorance.

10. Most joyful the Poet be;
It is through him that all men see.

11. Men are never very wise or select in the exercise of a new power.

12. No man should part with his own individuality and become that of another.

13. War will never yield but to the principles of universal justice and love.

14. The office of government is not to confer happiness, but to give men opportunity to work out happiness for themselves.

15. I see the marks of God in the heavens and the earth; but how much more in a liberal intellect, in magnanimity, in unconquerable rectitude, in a philanthropy which forgives every wrong, and which never despairs of the cause of Christ and human virtue: I do and I must reverence human nature. I bless it for its kind affections. I honor it for its achievements in science and art, and still more for its examples of heroic and saintly virtue. These are marks of a divine origin and the pledges of a celestial inheritance; and I thank God that my own lot is bound up with that of the human race.   *Inscription: Channing Memorial Public Garden, Boston*

W. M. PAXTON (1781–1840)

THIS prophet of progress spoke and wrote little, but for a period held his own with the spokesmen of change in his day.

Ideas are booming through the world louder than cannon. Thoughts are mightier than armies. Principles have achieved more victories than horsemen and chariots.

DANIEL WEBSTER (1782–1852)

THERE was scarcely a single great debate or controversy in the United States between 1812 and 1852 that did not draw eloquent comment— always on the side of union, freedom and national as opposed to sectional interest—from Webster, successively Representative, Senator and Secretary of State. He belonged to that fortunate minority of men (the makers of great quotations) who not only spoke clearly and graphically, but whose words carry the same eloquence in the reading. His collected writings, edited in 1903, fill eighteen large volumes.

1. Whatever makes men good Christians, makes them good citizens.

2. If there be anything in my style of thought to be commended, the credit is due to my kind parents in instilling into my mind an early love of the Scriptures.

3. A solemn and religious regard to spiritual and eternal things is an indispensable element of all true greatness.

4. Mind is the great lever of all things, . . .

5. Knowledge, in truth, is the great sun in the firmament. Life and power are scattered with all its beams.

6. Failure is more frequently from want of energy than from want of capital.

7. Falsehoods not only disagree with truths, but usually quarrel among themselves.

8. What is valuable is not new, and what is new is not valuable.

9. Let our object be our country, our whole country and nothing but our country.

Address at the Laying of the Cornerstone of the Bunker Hill Monument, 1825

10. Sink or swim, live or die, survive or perish, I give my hand and heart to this vote.

Discourse in Commemoration of Adams and Jefferson

11. Washington—a fixed star in the firmament of great names, shining without winking or obscuration, with clear, beneficent light. . . . America has furnished to the world the character of Washington. And if our American institutions had done nothing else, that alone would have entitled them to the respect of mankind.

12. It is my living sentiment, and by the blessing of God it shall be my dying sentiment,—Independence now and Independence forever.   *Ibid.*

13. One country, one constitution, one destiny.

14. There are persons who constantly clamor. They complain of oppression, speculation, and pernicious influence of wealth. They cry out loudly against all banks and corporations, and a means by which small capitalists become united in order to produce important and beneficial results. They carry on mad hostility against all established institutions. They would choke the fountain of human civilization.

15. When tillage begins, other arts follow. The farmers therefore are the founders of human civilization.

16. Justice, Sir, is the great interest of man on earth.

17. Liberty exists in proportion to wholesome restraint.

18. Labor in this country is independent and proud. It has not to ask the patronage of capital, but capital solicits the aid of labor.

19. The people's government, made for the people, made by the people, and answerable to the people.

20. When my eyes shall be turned to behold, for the last time, the sun in heaven, may I not see him shining on the broken and dishonored fragments of a once glorious Union; on States dissevered, discordant, belligerent, in a land rent with civil feuds, or drenched, it may be, in fraternal blood.

21. Liberty *and* Union, now and forever, one and inseparable!

22. God grants liberty only to those who love it, and are always ready to guard and defend it.

23. Inconsistencies of opinion, arising from changes of circumstances, are often justifiable.

24. I was born an American; I live an American; I shall die an American.

25. There is no refuge from confession but suicide; and suicide is confession.

26. There is nothing so powerful as truth,—and often nothing so strange.

27. If we work upon marble it will perish; if we work upon brass, time will efface it; if we rear temples, they will crumble into dust; but if we work upon immortal minds, if we imbue them with principles, with just the fear of God and love of our fellow-men, we engrave on those tablets something which will brighten all eternity.

28. A sense of duty pursues us ever. It is omnipresent, like the Deity. If we take to ourselves the wings of the morning, and dwell in the uttermost parts of the sea, duty performed or duty violated is still with us, for our happiness or our misery. If we say the darkness shall cover us, in the darkness as in the light our obligations are yet with us.

29. Philosophical argument, especially that drawn from the vastness of the universe, in comparison with the apparent insignificance of this globe, has sometimes shaken my reason for the faith which is in me; but my heart has always assured me that the gospel of Jesus Christ must be Divine Reality. The Sermon on the Mount cannot be a mere human production. This belief enters into the very depth of my conscience. The whole history of man proves it.

His epitaph, dictated the day before he died

WASHINGTON IRVING (1783–1859)

IRVING is generally regarded as the first American writer to be judged "great" by European critics. His most popular works, "Rip Van Winkle" and "The Legend of Sleepy Hollow" first appeared serially; their publication in book form made him the toast of the Continent and a favorite at home. Irving might never have made writing his profession but for the failure in his young manhood of a hardware business owned by his family. It is said that Sir Walter Scott, the British author, first encouraged him to take up writing seriously.

1. There is a certain relief in change, even though it be from bad to worse; as I have found in travelling in a stage-coach, that it is often a comfort to shift one's position and be bruised in a new place.

2. There is a healthful hardiness about real dignity that never dreads contact and communion with others, however humble.

3. There was one species of government under which he [Rip Van Winkle] had long groaned, and that was petticoat government.

4. The idol of to-day pushes the hero of yesterday out of our recollection; and will, in turn, be supplanted by his successor of to-morrow.

5. Man passes away; his name perishes from record and recollection; his history is as a tale that is told, and his very monument becomes a ruin.

6. Little minds are tamed and subdued by misfortune; but great minds rise above it.

7. The almighty dollar, that great object of universal devotion throughout our land, seems to have no genuine devotees in these peculiar villages. *Creole Village*

8. History fades into fable; fact becomes clouded with doubt and controversy; the inscription moulders from the tablet; the statue falls from the pedestal. Columns, arches, pyramids, what are they but heaps of sand; and their epitaphs, but characters written in the dust?

9. Here's to your good health and your family's good health, and may you all live long and prosper.

SAMUEL WOODWORTH (1784–1842)

A young editor in New York in 1823, Woodworth apparently suffered a touch of nostalgia for his boyhood home, in Scituate, Massachusetts and wrote a little poem. It is his most enduring work, having outlasted his play *The Forest Rose*, which set a record for longevity.

> How dear to this heart are the scenes of my childhood,
>   When fond recollections presents them to view.
>
>   .   .   .   .
>
> Then soon with the emblem of truth overflowing,
>   And dripping with coolness, it rose from the
>   well.
>
>   .   .   .   .
>
> The old oaken bucket, the iron-bound bucket,
>   The moss-covered bucket, which hung in the well.
>
> *The Old Oaken Bucket*

OLIVER HAZARD PERRY (1785–1819)

THERE have been few historic naval battles as limited as the one fought on Lake Erie, September 10, 1813, between two small and locally built squadrons of ships destined to fight for control of the Great Western Basin of the United States in the War of 1812. Perry overcame his British adversary, although he had to abandon his own sinking flagship during the fight and transfer to another. His report, written at 4:00 P.M. made history and established his immortality.

We have met the enemy and they are ours.

RICHARD HENRY DANA (1787–1879)

DANA, as editorial associate of the "North American Review," was considered one of the first of the great American critics. His essays were collected in 1850 before he began a long retirement.

1. O sin, what hast thou done to this fair earth!

2. Better to be driven out from among men than to be disliked of children.

3. A voice within us speaks the startling word, "Man, thou shalt never die!"

4. Patient endurance of sufferings, bold resistance of power, forgiveness of injuries, hard-tried and faithful friendship, and self-sacrificing love, are seen in beautiful relief over the flat uniformity of life, or stand out in steady and bright grandeur in the midst of the dark deeds of men.

5. It is an impression, of which we can not rid ourselves, if we would, when sitting by the body of a friend, that he still has a consciousness of our presence; that, though he no longer has a concern in the common things of the world, love and thought are still there. The face which we had been familiar with so long, when it was all life and motion, seems only in a state of rest. We know not how to make it real to ourselves that in the body before us there is not a something still alive.

SARAH JOSEPHA (BUELL) HALE (1788–1879)

MRS. Hale, a widow with five children to support, originally went to work as a writer and was an editor of women's magazines, notably *Godey's Lady's Book* (which she started), for almost forty years. But a verse published in her *Poems for Our Children,* 1830 about a lamb [her authorship is disputed] is her monument.

> Mary had a little lamb,
>   Its fleece was white as snow,
> And everywhere that Mary went
>   The lamb was sure to go. . . .
>
> *Mary's Lamb*

HANNAH FLAGG GOULD (1789–1865)

A popular poet for twenty years Hannah Gould is best remembered for her neatly turned comment on the transience of life.

Alone I walked the ocean strand,
    A pearly shell was in my hand;
I stooped and wrote upon the sand
    My name—the year—the day.

.   .   .   .

As onward from the spot I passed,
    One lingering look behind I cast,
A wave came rolling high and fast,
    And washed my lines away.

A Name on the Sand

FITZ-GREENE HALLECK
(1790–1867)

IN 1823, a Greek patriot named Marco Bozzaris was killed in an attack on Turkish forces in Greece. On that event, Halleck, a noted poet and satirist, wrote a poem of dramatic intensity, quite different from his other more homely works. Its stirring words live in our memory.

1. Strike—till the last armed foe expires;
    Strike—for your altars and your fires;
    Strike—for the green graves of your sires;
        God—and your native land! . . .

Marco Bozzaris

2. They love their land, because it is their own,
        And scorn to give aught other reason why;
    Would shake hands with a king upon his throne,
        And think it kindness to his majesty.

Connecticut

JOHN HOWARD PAYNE (1791–1852)

DO you recall the operetta by Payne, an actor and playwright, entitled *Clari, or the Maid of Milan?* Probably not, but who has not sung the long-lived and sentimental hit from it?

'Mid pleasures and palaces though we may roam,
Be it ever so humble, there's no place like home;
A charm from the sky seems to hallow us there,
Which, seek through the world, is ne'er met with else-
	where.

	. . . .

An exile from home, splendor dazzles in vain;
Oh, give me my lowly thatched cottage again!
The birds singing gayly, that came at my call,—
Give me them,—and the peace of mind, dearer than all!

Home, Sweet Home

CHARLES SPRAGUE (1791–1875)

SPRAGUE was a banker, and a prominent one, in New York, in an age when there was little intercourse between such "solid citizens" and literary figures. Sprague, a published poet, bridged the gap for he belonged to the worlds of both finance and literature.

1. Lo, where the Stage, the poor, degraded Stage,
	Holds its warped mirror to a gaping age!

Curiosity

2. Yes, social friend, I love thee well,
	In learned doctors' spite;
	Thy clouds all other clouds dispel
	And lap me in delight.

To My Cigar

WILLIAM CULLEN BRYANT (1794–1878)

IT is another paradox that the beloved Bryant, who was to become America's first major poet, wrote poetry as a kind of hobby during a long career bristling with the mundane cares, first, of a lawyer, and afterward of a newspaper editor militantly espousing free trade and abolition of slavery. Some of his best-known works, including "Thanatopsis" and "To a Waterfowl," were composed before he was twenty-one and established an early reputation for him.

1. Eloquence is the poetry of prose.
2. Here the free spirit of mankind, at length,
      Throws its last fetters off; and who shall place
   A limit to the giant's unchained strength,
      Or curb his swiftness in the forward race?

The Ages

3. To him who in the love of Nature holds
      Communion with her visible forms, she speaks
   A various language;

.   .   .

   Go forth, under the open sky, and list
      To Nature's teachings,

.   .   .

                          The hills
   Rock-ribbed and ancient as the sun,—

.   .   .

                       All that tread
   The globe are but a handful to the tribes
   That slumber in its bosom

.   .   .

   So live, that when thy summons comes to join
      The innumerable caravan, which moves
   To that mysterious realm, where each shall take
      His chamber in the silent halls of death,
   Thou go not, like the quarry-slave at night,
      Scourged to his dungeon, but, sustained and soothed
   By an unfaltering trust, approach thy grave,
      Like one that wraps the drapery of his couch
   About him, and lies down to pleasant dreams.

Thanatopsis

4.   Vainly the fowler's eye
      Might mark thy distant flight to do thee wrong,

As, darkly painted on the crimson sky,
   Thy figure floats along.

.   .   .   .

He who, from zone to zone,
Guides through the sky thy certain flight,
In the long way that I must tread alone,
   Will lead my steps aright.

To a Waterfowl

5. The moon is at her full, and riding high,
      Floods the calm fields with light.
   The airs that hover in the summer sky
      Are all asleep to-night.

The Tides

6. The stormy March is come at last,
      With wind, and cloud, and changing skies;
   I hear the rushing of the blast,
      That through the snowy valley flies.

March

7. The groves were God's first temples, Ere man learned
      To hew the shaft, and lay the architrave,
   And spread the roof above them,—ere he framed
      The lofty vault, to gather and roll back
   The sound of anthems; in the darkling wood
      Amidst the cool and silence, he knelt down
   And offered to the Mightiest solemn thanks.
      And supplication.

.   .   .   .

Ah, why
Should we, in the world's riper years, neglect
God's ancient sanctuaries, and adore
   Only among the crowd and under roofs
That our frail hands have raised?

A Forest Hymn

8. The melancholy days are come, the saddest of the year,
      Of wailing winds, and naked woods, and meadows
         brown and sere.

The Death of the Flowers

9. Loveliest of lovely things are they
      On earth that soonest pass away.
   The rose that lives its little hour
      Is prized beyond the sculptured flower.

A Scene on the Banks of the Hudson

10. These are the gardens of the Desert, these
       The unshorn fields, boundless and beautiful,
    For which the speech of England has no name—
       The Prairies.

The Prairies

11. Truth crushed to earth shall rise again;
       Th' eternal years of God are hers;
    But Error, wounded, writhes in pain,
       And dies among his worshippers.

The Battle Field

12. The summer day is closed, the sun is set:
       Well they have done their office, those bright hours,
    The latest of whose train goes softly out
       In the red west.

                .   .   .   .

    There is a day of sunny rest
    For every dark and troubled night;
    And grief may hide an evening guest,
    But joy shall come with early light.

                .   .   .   .

                Man foretells afar
    The courses of the stars; the very hour
    He knows when they shall darken or grow bright;
    Yet doth the eclipse of Sorrow and of Death
    Come unforewarned.

An Evening Revery

13. Lord, who ordainest for mankind
       Benignant toils and tender cares:
    We thank thee for the ties that bind
       The mother to the child she bears.

The Mother's Hymn

14.   A sculptor wields
The chisel, and the stricken marble grows
To beauty.

The Flood of Years

15. A breeze came wandering from the sky,
        Light as the whispers of a dream, . . .

The Wind and Stream

16. The little windflower, whose just opened eye
        Is blue as the spring heaven it gazes at.

.   .   .   .

        Look! the massy trunks
Are cased in the pure crystal; each light spray,
        Nodding and tinkling in the breath of heaven,
Is studded with its trembling water-drops,
        That glimmer with an amesthystine light.

A Winter Piece

17. No trumpet blast profaned
        The hour in which the Prince of Peace was born;
No bloody streamlet stained
        Earth's silver rivers on that sacred morn.

Christmas in 1875

EDWARD EVERETT (1794–1865)

IN sheer oratorical power, Edward Everett's talents equalled and possibly exceeded those of his friend Daniel Webster. In fact this reputation has overshadowed the other rather solid achievements of his lifetime, including congressional service, the presidency of Harvard University, and a term as Secretary of State under Fillmore. The greatest irony in his career was that it was he who delivered the "oration" at the dedication of Gettysburg— a speech completely overshadowed in history by President Lincoln's brief address.

1. When I am dead, no pageant train
        Shall waste their sorrows at my bier,

> Nor worthless pomp of homage vain
> Stain it with hypocritic tear.
>
> *Alaric the Visigoth*

2. No gilded dome swells from the lowly roof to catch the morning or evening beam; but the love and gratitude of united America settle upon it in one eternal sunshine. From beneath that humble roof went forth the intrepid and unselfish warrior, the magistrate who knew no glory but his country's good; to that he returned, happiest when his work was done. There he lived in noble simplicity, there he died in glory and peace. While it stands, the latest generations of the grateful children of America will make this pilgrimage to it as to a shrine; and when it shall fall, if fall it must, the name and the memory of Washington shall shed an eternal glory on the spot. *Oration on the Character of Washington*

3. The days of palmy prosperity are not those most favorable to the display of public virtue or the influence of wise and good men. In hard, doubtful, unprosperous, and dangerous times, the disinterested and patriotic find their way, by a species of public interest, unopposed, joyfully welcomed, to the control of affairs.

Mount Vernon Papers

4. The faithful marble may preserve their image; the engraven brass may proclaim their worth; but the humblest sod of Independent America, with nothing but the dew-drops of the morning to gild it, is a prouder mausoleum than kings or conquerors can boast. The country is their monument. Its independence is their epitaph.

Memorial address honoring John Adams and Thomas Jefferson

JOSEPH RODMAN DRAKE (1795–1820)

THE dates above are correct; Drake laid a firm reputation as poet and satirist in only twenty-five years of life. With his friend Fitz-Greene Halleck he wrote the humorous "Croaker Papers."

The composition quoted in part here, was for a century [and even occasionally is now] a favorite "recitation."

When Freedom from her mountain-height
    Unfurled her standard in the air,
She tore the azure robe of night,
    And set the stars of glory there.
She mingled with its gorgeous dykes
    The milky baldric of the sky,
And striped its pure, celestial white
    With streakings of the morning light.

Flag of the free heart's hope and home!
    By angel hands to valour given;
Thy stars have lit the welkin dome,
    And all thy hues were born in heaven.
Forever float that standard sheet!
    Where breathes the foe but falls before us;
With Freedom's soil beneath our feet,
    And Freedom's banner streaming o'er us?

The American Flag

JOSIAH TATTNALL (1795–1871)

TO this naval officer is attributed a famous proverb. When called upon to explain why, in 1850, he assisted British and French naval units in shelling Chinese forts during a local dispute (thus breaching his country's neutrality), Tattnall is said to have exclaimed:

Blood is thicker than water.

HORACE MANN (1796–1859)

AFTER Horace Mann's death, the American public awoke to the accomplishment of this great American educator who had sparked the improvement of public schools in America. On the surface Mann's career seems hardly spectacular. After working his way through Brown University, he practiced law, did a stint in politics and then for twelve years was secretary of the Massachusetts State Board of Education, a term which saw considerable educational reform. At his death he was a teacher of theology and philosophy at Antioch College. It was his works and words, subsequently collected by biographers, that proved him the greatest spur to developments in education.

1. Schoolhouses are the republican line of fortifications.

2. Education is our only political safety.

3. A teacher who is attempting to teach without inspiring the pupil with a desire to learn is hammering on a cold iron.

4. Genius may conceive, but patient labor must consummate.

5. It is more difficult, and calls for higher energies of soul, to live a martyr than to die one.

6. To pity distress is but human; to relieve it is Godlike.

7. Unfaithfulness in the keeping of an appointment is an act of clear dishonesty. You may as well borrow a person's money as his time.

8. Lost, yesterday, somewhere between sunrise and sunset, two golden hours, each set with sixty diamond minutes. No reward is offered, for they are gone forever.

(AMOS) BRONSON ALCOTT (1799–1888)

NOW known primarily as the father of Louisa May Alcott, this self-taught Connecticut Yankee pursued the dual careers of educational reformer and transcendental philosopher, winning an international reputation but never financially secure until his daughter became a literary success. He founded Boston's famous Trinity School.

1. Many can argue; not many converse.

2. Egotists cannot converse, they talk only to themselves.

3. I consider it the best part of an education to have been born and brought up in the country.

4. Madame de Staël pronounced architecture to be frozen music; so is statuary crystallized spirituality.

5. The great teacher defends his pupils against his own per-

sonal influence. He inspires self-distrust. He guides their eyes from him to the spirit that quickens him. He will have no disciple.

6. One's outlook is a part of his virtue.

7. . . . the deepest truths are best read between the lines, and, for the most part, refuse to be written.

8. Nature is thought immersed in matter.

9. Who loves a garden still his Eden keeps,
Perennial pleasures plants, and wholesome harvests reaps.

Tablets

10. I press thee to my heart as Duty's faithful child.

Sonnet to Louisa May Alcott

RUFUS CHOATE (1799–1859)

ANOTHER product of Massachusetts, Choate ranked as orator, Congressman and lawyer virtually alongside Webster and Everett, but his contribution was the pithy statement rather than the rolling phrase.

1. Neither irony nor sarcasm is argument.

2. A book is the only immortality.

3. The courage of New England was the "courage of Conscience." It did not rise to that insane and awful passion, the love of war for itself.

4. The final end of Government is not to exercise restraint but to do good.

5. We join ourselves to no party that does not carry the flag and keep step to the music of the Union.

Letter to a Worcester Whig Convention, 1855

DAVID GLASGOW FARRAGUT (1801–1870)

COMMODORE Farragut's squadron was about to fight its way into heavily defended Mobile May, August 5, 1864. Warned of the risk to his ships, he gave but one dramatic order.

Damn the torpedoes! Captain Drayton, go ahead!

WILLIAM HENRY SEWARD (1801–1872)

SEWARD who, as Lincoln's Secretary of State, was savagely attacked but recovered on the night his President was assassinated, will be best remembered for "Seward's Folly": purchase of Alaska from Russia in 1867. But as a Senator before the Civil War, he made in abolitionist speeches, two statements that became northern slogans.

    1. There is a higher law than the Constitution.

    2. It [the slavery/anti-slavery contest] is an irrepressible conflict between opposing and enduring forces.

GEORGE POPE MORRIS (1802–1864)

POET and journalist, Morris founded the literary weekly *New-York Mirror* and, among others, helped to make Bryant's readership. He enjoyed his own following, however, won by a versatility of subject matter which ranged from his famous "tree" to political themes.

    1. Woodman, spare that tree!
        Touch not a single bough!
    In youth it sheltered me,
        And I'll protect it now.

Woodman, Spare That Tree

    2. The union of lakes—the union of lands,
        The union of States none can sever,
    The union of hearts, the union of hands,
        And the flag of our Union forever.

The Flag of Our Union

    3. Near the lake where drooped the willow,
        Long time ago.

Near the Lake

RALPH WALDO EMERSON
(1803–1882)

EMERSON is one of America's most forceful advocates of the dignity of man. A poor scholar as a Harvard undergraduate, suffering from poor health and finally losing his first and only pastorate, of Old North Church in Boston, at the age of thirty he went to England to reorient himself. His espousal of transcendentalism caused a break with Harvard, but as he matured Emerson began publishing his poetry, established great popularity with lectures and in turn published his lectures in book form, a legacy of wisdom to future generations. He is among the half dozen most quoted men in America today.

1. How cunningly nature hides every wrinkle of inconceivable antiquity under roses and violets and morning dew.

2. Nature abhors the old.

3. The first farmer was the first man, and all historic nobility rests on possession and use of land.

4. Hitch your wagon to a star.

5. America is a country of young men.

6. No sensible person ever made an apology.

7. The silence that accepts merit as the most natural thing in the world, is the highest applause.

8. Every artist was first an amateur.

9. God may forgive sins, he said, but awkwardness has no forgiveness in heaven or earth.

10. Belief consists in accepting the affirmations of the soul; Unbelief in denying them.

11. The [Bible] comes with a certain official claim against which the mind revolts. The book has its own nobilities—might well be charming, if it was left simply on its merits, as the others; but this 'you must'—'it is your duty,' repels. 'Tis like the introduction of martial law into Concord.

12. Every burned book enlightens the world.

13. Cities force growth, and make men talkative and entertaining, but they make them artificial.

14. A sufficient measure of civilization is the influence of good women.

15. We think our civilization near its meridian, but we are yet only at the cock-crowing and the morning star.

16. I always seem to suffer some loss of faith on entering cities.

17. The truest test of civilization is not the census, nor the size of cities, nor the crops; no, but the kind of man the country turns out.

18. Curses may recoil on the head of him who imprecates them. If you put a chain around the neck of a slave the other end fastens itself around your own.

19. We are reformers in spring and summer; in autumn and winter we stand by the old; reformers in the morning, conservers at night. Reform is affirmative, conservatism negative; conservatism goes for comfort, reform for truth.

20. A foolish consistency is the hobgoblin of little minds, adored by little statesmen and philosophers and divines.

21. Speak what you think to-day in words as hard as cannon-balls, and to-morrow speak what to-morrow thinks in hard words again, though it contradict everything you said to-day.

22. Conversation is the laboratory and workshop of the student.

23. Life is not so short but that there is always time enough for courtesy.

24. Culture, with us, ends in headache.

25. Wilt thou seal up the avenues of ill?
Pay every debt as if God wrote the bill.

26. Discontent is the want of self-reliance; it is the infirmity of will.

27. Vigor is contagious; and whatever makes us either think or feel strongly adds to our power and enlarges our field of action.

28. The things taught in schools and colleges are not an education, but the means of education.

29. Nothing great was ever achieved without enthusiasm.

30. There can be no excess to love, none to knowledge, none to beauty, when these attributes are considered in the purest sense.

31. An eye can threaten like a loaded and levelled gun, or can

insult like hissing or kicking; or, in its altered mood, by beams of kindness, it can make the heart dance with joy.

32. All I have seen teaches me to trust the Creator for all I have not seen.

33. Fear always springs from ignorance.

34. His heart was as great as the world, but there was no room in it to hold the memory of a wrong.

35. A friend may well be reckoned the masterpiece of nature.

36. The only way to have a friend is to be one.

37. The highest compact we can make with our fellow is,—Let there be truth between us two forevermore.

38. The flowering of civilization is the finished man, the man of sense, of grace, of accomplishment, of social power—the gentleman.

39. Nature never sends a great man into the planet, without confiding the secret to another soul.

40. The first wealth is health.

41. Every hero becomes a bore at last.

42. Every man is a hero and an oracle to somebody, and to that person whatever he says has an enhanced value.

43. There is properly no history; only biography.

44. Let not the emphasis of hospitality lie in bed and board; but let truth and love and honor and courtesy flow in all thy deeds.

45. Science does not know its debt to imagination. Goethe did not believe that a great naturalist could exist without this faculty.

46. Nature is methodical, and doeth her work well. Time is never to be hurried.

47. An institution is the lengthened shadow of one man.

48. Works of the intellect are great only by comparison with each other.

49. Our knowledge is the amassed thought and experience of innumerable minds.

50. If you would lift me you must be on higher ground.

51. Light is the first of painters. There is no object so foul that intense light will not make it beautiful.

52. All mankind love a lover.

53. Man is a piece of the universe made alive.

54. Life is not so short that there is not always time enough for courtesy.

55. Fine manners need the support of fine manners in others.

56. Is not marriage an open question, when it is alleged, from the beginning of the world, that such as are in the institution wish to get out, and such as are out wish to get in?

57. The mob is man voluntarily descending to the nature of the beast.

58. Men are what their mothers made them.

59. Obedience alone gives the right to command.

60. The crowning fortune of a man is to be born to some pursuit which finds him employment and happiness, whether it be to make baskets, or broadswords, or candles, or statues, or songs.

61. Nature is upheld by antagonisms. Passions, resistance, danger, are educators. We acquire the strength we have overcome.

62. Adopt the pace of nature; her secret is patience.

63. When Shakespeare is charged with debts to his authors, Landor replies, "Yet he was more original than his originals. He breathed upon dead bodies and brought them into life."

64. The finest poetry was first experience.

65. The greatest man in history was the poorest.

66. Concentration is the secret of strength in politics, in war, in trade, in short, in all management of human affairs.

67. Next to the originator of a good sentence is the first quoter of it.

68. I should as soon think of swimming across the Charles River when I wish to go to Boston, as of reading all my books in originals, when I have them rendered for me in my mother tongue.

69. Ah, if the rich were as rich as the poor fancy riches!

70. Steam is no stronger now than it was a hundred years ago, but it is put to better use.

71. The shoemaker makes a good shoe because he makes nothing else.

72. Nothing is more simple than greatness; indeed, to be simple is to be great.

73. I do not see how a barbarous community and a civilized community can constitute a state. I think we must get rid of slavery or we must get rid of freedom.

74. The one thing in the world, of value, is the active soul.

75. Speech is power: speech is to persuade, to convert, to compel.

76. If a man write a better book, preach a better sermon, or make a better mouse-trap, than his neighbor, tho' he build his house in the woods, the world will make a beaten path to his door.

77. Every sweet hath its sour, every evil its good.

78. Write it in your heart that every day is the best day in the year. No man has learned anything rightly, until he knows that every day is Doomsday.

79. He that despiseth small things will perish little by little.

80. Trust men, and they will be true to you; treat them greatly, and they will show themselves great.

81. There is always safety in valor.

82. Without a rich heart wealth is an ugly beggar.

83. Men love to wonder and that is the seed of science.

84. And what greater calamity can fall upon a nation than the loss of worship?

85. There is no luck in literary reputation. They who make up the final verdict upon every book are not the partial and noisy readers of the hour when it appears; but a court as of angels, a public not to be bribed, not to be entreated, and not to be over-awed, decides upon every man's title and fame.

86. I like a church; I like a cowl;
      I love a prophet of the soul;
   And on my heart monastic aisles
      Fall like sweet strains, or pensive smiles:
   Yet not for all his faith can see
      Would I that cowlèd churchman be.

               .   .   .   .

   Not from a vain or shallow thought
      His awful Jove young Phidias brought;

               .   .   .   .

   The hand that rounded Peter's dome,
      And groined the aisles of Christian Rome,
   Wrought in a sad sincerity;
      Himself from God he could not free;

He builded better than he knew;—
The conscious stone to beauty grew.

. . . .

Earth proudly wears the Parthenon,
As the best gem upon her zone, ...

The Problem

87. Good-bye, proud world! I'm going home;
Thou art not my friend, and I'm not thine.

. . . .

Oh, when I am safe in my sylvan home,
I tread on the pride of Greece and Rome;
And when I am stretched beneath the pines
Where the evening star so holy shines,
I laugh at the lore and the pride of man,
At the sophist schools and the learned clan;
For what are they all in their high conceit,
When man in the bush with God may meet.

Good-Bye

88. Let me go where'er I will,
I hear a sky-born music still.

. . . .

But in the mud and scum of things
There always, always something sings.

Fragments

89. By the rude bridge that arched the flood,
Their flag to April's breeze unfurl'd;
Here once the embattl'd farmers stood,
And fired the shot heard round the world.

*Hymn sung at the dedication of the
Concord Battle Monument, April 19, 1836*

90. So nigh is grandeur to our dust,
So near is God to man,
When Duty whispers low, *Thou must,*
The youth replies, *I can.*

Voluntaries

91. He thought it happier to be dead,

    To die for Beauty, than live for bread.

                                    Ode to Beauty

92. Go where he will, the wise man is at home,
    His hearth the earth,—his hall the azure dome.

                                 Wood-Notes

93. In the vaunted works of Art,
    The master-stroke is Nature's part.

                                    Art

94. There is no great and no small
    To the Soul that maketh all:
And where it cometh all things are;
    And it cometh everywhere.

        .   .   .   .

I am the owner of the sphere,
    Of the seven stars and the solar year,
Of Caesar's hand, and Plato's brain,
    Of Lord Christ's heart, and Shakespeare's strain.

                                 History

95. He who has a thousand friends has not a friend to spare,
    And he who has one enemy will meet him everywhere.

                              Translation

96. We grant no dukedoms to the few,
    We hold like rights and shall;
Equal on Sunday in the pew,
    On Monday in the mall.
For what avail the plough or sail
    Or land, or life, if freedom fail?

                                 Boston

NATHANIEL HAWTHORNE (1804–1864)

THIS native of Salem, Massachusetts and student at Bowdoin, had to wait until his mid-thirties for any serious recognition, which came with publication of some short stories, "Twice-Told Tales," although he won the friendship of Emerson, Thoreau and Herman Melville. He was past forty, holding a public job to earn a living, when he began *The Scarlet Letter,* to be followed by other famous works including his favorite, *The House of the Seven Gables.* Thereafter his production was massive. Few American authors have enjoyed as many editions or been the subject of as many biographies.

1. Death possesses a good deal of real estate, namely the graveyard in every town.

2. Every individual has a place to fill in the world, and is important in some respect, whether he chooses to be so or not.

3. Caresses, expressions of one sort or another, are necessary to the life of the affections as leaves are to the life of a tree. If they are wholly restrained love will die at the roots.

4. Language—human language—after all, is but little better than the croak and cackle of fowls, and other utterances of brute nature—sometimes not so adequate.

5. Of a bitter satirist it might be said that the person or thing on which his satire fell shriveled up as if the devil had spit on it.

6. Sleeping or waking, we hear not the airy footsteps of the strange things that almost happen.   *1–6: Twice-Told Tales*

7. Our Creator would never have made such lovely days, and have given us the deep hearts to enjoy them, above and beyond all thought, unless we were meant to be immortal.

Mosses from an Old Manse

8. Some maladies are rich and precious and only to be acquired by the right of inheritance or purchased with gold.

9. She poured out the liquid music of her voice to quench the thirst of her spirit.

10. Human nature will not flourish, any more than a potato, if it be planted and replanted, for too long a series of generations, in the same worn-out soil.

11. Neither the front nor the back entrance of the Custom-House opens on the road to Paradise.

12. It is a good lesson—though it may often be a hard one—for a man who has dreamed of literary fame, [and of making for himself a rank among the world's dignitaries by such means,] to

step aside out of the narrow circle in which his claims are recognized, and to find how utterly devoid of significance, beyond that circle, is all that he achieves, and all he aims at.

13. The black flower of civilized society, a prison.

14. On the breast of her gown, in red cloth, surrounded with an elaborate embroidery and fantastic flourishes of gold-thread, appeared the letter A.

15. She named the infant "Pearl," as being of great price,— purchased with all she had.

16. It is to the credit of human nature, that, except where its selfishness is brought into play, it loves more readily than it hates.

17. Let men tremble to win the hand of woman, unless they win along with it the utmost passion of her heart.

18. No man, for any considerable period, can wear one face to himself, and another to the multitude, without finally getting bewildered as to which may be the true.

8–18: The Scarlet Letter

19. Life is made up of marble and mud.

20. Providence seldom vouchsafes to mortals any more than just that degree of encouragement which suffices to keep them at a reasonably full exertion of their powers.

21. A stale article, if you dip it in a good, warm, sunny smile, will go off better than a fresh one that you've scowled upon.

22. Life, within doors, has few pleasanter prospects than a neatly arranged and well-provisioned breakfast-table.

23. What other dungeon is so dark as one's own heart!

24. Once in every half-century, at longest, a family should be merged into the great, obscure mass of humanity, and forget all about its ancestors.

25. The world owes all of its onward impulses to men ill at ease. The happy man inevitably confines himself within ancient limits.

26. Of all the events which constitute a person's biography, there is scarcely one . . . to which the world so easily reconciles itself as to his death.   *19–26: The House of the Seven Gables*

27. It is a token of healthy and gentle characteristics, when women of high thoughts and accomplishments love to sew; es-

pecially as they are never more at home with their own hearts than while so occupied.

28. One picture in ten thousand, perhaps, ought to live in the applause of mankind, from generation to generation until the colors fade and blacken out of sight or the canvas rots entirely away.

29. We do ourselves wrong, and too meanly estimate the holiness about us, when we deem that any act or enjoyment good in itself, is not good to do religiously.

30. Rome? The city of all time, and of all the world!

31. Every young sculptor seems to think that he must give the world some specimen of indecorous womanhood, and call it Eve, Venus, a Nymph, or any name that may apologize for a lack of decent clothing.

32. At no time are people so sedulously careful to keep their trifling appointments, attend to their ordinary occupations, and thus put a commonplace aspect on life, as when conscious of some secret that if suspected would make them look monstrous in the general eye.

33. Nobody, I think, ought to read poetry, or look at pictures or statues, who cannot find a great deal more in them than the poet or artist has actually expressed.   *27–33: The Marble Faun*

34. Mountains are earth's undecaying monuments.

Sketches from Memory

35. It is not the statesman, the warrior, or the monarch that survives, but the despised poet, whom they may have fed with their crumbs, and to whom they owe all that they now are or have —a name.   *Up the Thames*

IRA FREDERICK ALDRIDGE (c. 1805–1867)

THE brief records recount Aldridge as having enjoyed an unusual fame for his race, in his day, as he is described as a "Negro tragedian." But that he was more than an actor is shown by a couplet.

The bow is bent, the arrow flies,
    The winged shaft of fate.

On William Tell

WILLIAM LLOYD GARRISON
(1805–1879)

GARRISON is well known and often quoted for his fiery words in favor of the abolition of slavery, which appeared in his small newspaper, *The Liberator*. But he made all types of enemies by his equal opposition to force, including the Civil War itself, until Lincoln issued the Emancipation Proclamation. His other crusades were in favor of woman suffrage, fair treatment for Indians, and prohibition.

1. I am in earnest.—I will not equivocate—I will not excuse —I will not retreat a single inch—and I will be heard!
    First issue of The Liberator, Jan. 1, 1831

2. My country is the world; my countrymen are mankind.
    Prospectus of the Public Liberator, 1830

3. I will be as harsh as truth and as uncompromising as justice.   *The Liberator, 1831*

4. The compact which exists between the North and the South is a covenant with death and an agreement with hell.
    Resolution written for, and adopted by the Anti-Slavery Society, Jan. 27, 1843

5. With reasonable men, I will reason; with humane men, I will plead; but to tyrants I will give no quarter, nor waste arguments where they will certainly be lost.

    Life

6. Since the creation of the world there has been no tyrant like Intemperance, and no slaves so cruelly treated as his.

7. We may be personally defeated, but our principles never.

8. Wherever there is a human being, I see God-given rights inherent in the being, whatever may be the sex or the complexion.

9. The success of any great moral enterprise does not depend upon numbers.

10. You cannot possibly have a broader basis for any government than that which includes all the people, with all their rights in their hands, and with an equal power to maintain their rights.

SIDNEY SHERMAN (1805–1873)

WHILE battles by debates over the Union were being fought in the East, the war of Texas for independence from Mexico saw the massacre at the Alamo. A three-word battlecry uttered at San Jacinto by the Texas commander of April 21, 1836 is immortal.

Remember the Alamo!

EDWIN FORREST (1806–1872)

AND from the world of the stage, the greatest tragedian of his time, commented, only too truly.

The actor's popularity is evanescent; applauded today, forgotten tomorrow.

WILLIAM GILMORE SIMMS (1806–1870)

THIS novelist and historian of his native South Carolina, whose popularity—even fame—vanished with the Civil War, left one eloquent statement on self-justification.

Better that we should err in action than wholly refuse to perform. The storm is so much better than the calm, as it declares the presence of a living principle. Stagnation is something worse than death. It is corruption also.

ELIZABETH OAKES SMITH
(1806–1893)

MRS. Smith, a spokeswoman for social and moral reform, achieved considerable success as the author of "dime novels" in her period. In an introspective moment she penned this verse.

> Faith is the subtle chain
>   Which binds us to the infinite; the voice
> Of a deep life within, that will remain
>   Until we crowd it thence.

Faith

NATHANIEL PARKER WILLIS
(1806–1867)

THIS writer, and in later life, editor of the *New York Evening Mirror,* wrote principally essays and verse of a rather shallow nature, but his collected works have yielded some memorable thoughts.

1. The innocence that feels no risk and is taught no caution is more vulnerable than guilt, and oftener assailed.
2. The sin forgiven by Christ in Heaven
       By man is cursed away.

Unseen Spirits

3. But he who never sins can little boast
       Compared to him who goes and sins no more!

The Lady Jane

JAMES HENRY HAMMOND
(1807–1864)

THIS senator from South Carolina, an avid secessionist, left a ringing phrase shouted in a speech to the Senate, in March, 1858.

Cotton is King!

HENRY WADSWORTH LONGFELLOW (1807–1882)

ALTHOUGH some modern commentators find him not quite substantial enough for their tastes, Longfellow is the prototype of a scholarly man. Born in Maine and graduated from Bowdoin (in the same class with Hawthorne) he studied in Europe, taught modern languages of which he mastered at least ten, first at Bowdoin and then at Harvard, until the demands of fame as a writer and a poet forced him to leave his academic work. He was a towering figure in nineteenth-century American letters. Notable excerpts from his works are the best proof of his metric genius and breadth of interest.

1. Most people would succeed in small things if they were not troubled with great ambitions.

2. Give what you have. To some one, it may be better than you dare think.

3. If we could read the secret history of our enemies, we should find in each man's life sorrow and suffering enough to disarm all hostilities.

4. All the means of action—the shapeless masses—the materials—lie everywhere about us; what we need is the celestial fire to change the flint into transparent crystal, bright and clear.

5. In this world a man must be either anvil or hammer.

6. A single conversation across the table with a wise man is better than ten years' study of books.

7. The young may die, but the old must!

8. We judge ourselves by what we feel capable of doing, while others judge us by what we have already done.

9. Every dew-drop and rain-drop had a whole heaven within it.

10. Fame comes only when deserved and then it is as inevitable as destiny, for it is destiny.

11. Well it has been said that there is no grief like the grief which does not speak.

12. The lowest ebb is the turn of the tide.

13. Morality without religion is only a kind of dead reckoning, —an endeavor to find our place on a cloudy sea by measuring the distance we have run, but without any observation of the heavenly bodies.

14. Music is the universal language of mankind.

15. There are no birds in last year's nests.

16. All things come round to him who will but wait.

17. Next to being a great poet is the power of understanding one.

18. Into each life some rain must fall.

19. Resolve, and thou art free.

20. As turning the logs will make a dull fire burn, so change of studies a dull brain.

21. A boy's will is the wind's will, . . .

22. Glorious indeed is the world of God around us, but more glorious the will of God within us. There lies the land of Song; there lies the poet's native land.

23. . . . I heard the trailing garments of the Night
    Sweep through her marble halls.

Hymn to Night

24. Tell me not, in mournful numbers,
    Life is but an empty dream!—
For the soul is dead that slumbers,
    And things are not what they seem.

Life is real! Life is earnest!
    And the grave is not its goal;
Dust thou art, to dust returnest,
    Was not spoken of the soul.

.   .   .   .

Art is long, and Time is fleeting,
    And our hearts, though stout and brave,
Still, like muffled dreams, are beating
    Funeral marches to the grave.

.   .   .   .

Trust no Future, howe'er pleasant!
Let the dead Past bury its dead!

Act—act in the living Present!
Heart within, and God o'erhead!

Lives of great men all remind us
We can make our lives sublime,
And, departing, leave behind us
Footprints on the sands of time;

.   .   .   .

Let us, then, be up and doing,
With a heart for any fate;
Still achieving, still pursuing,
Learn to labor and to wait.

A Psalm of Life

25. Spake full well, in language quaint and olden,
One who dwelled by the castled Rhine,
When he called the flowers, so blue and golden,
Stars, that in earth's firmament do shine

.   .   .   .

Gorgeous flowers in the sunlight shining,
Blossoms flaunting in the eye of day,
Tremulous leaves, with soft and silver lining,
Buds that open only to decay.

Flowers

26. Blue were her eyes as the fairy-flax,
Her cheeks like the dawn of the day,
And her bosom white as the hawthorn buds,
That ope in the month of May.

.   .   .   .

And fast through the midnight dark and drear,
Through the whistling sleet and snow,
Like a sheeted ghost, the vessel swept
Towards the reef of Norman's Woe

.   .   .   .

Christ save us all from a death like this,
On the reef of Norman's Woe!

The Wreck of the Hesperus

27. His brow is wet with honest sweat,
   He earns whate'er he can,
 And looks the whole world in the face
   For he owes not any man. . . .
Something attempted, something done,
   Has earned a night's repose.
         The Village Blacksmith

28. No one is so accursed by fate,
 No one so utterly desolate,
   But some heart, though unknown,
   Responds unto his own.
            Endymion

29. A banner with the strange device,
  Excelsior!
             Excelsior

30. Stars of the summer night!
   Far in yon azure deeps,
 Hide, hide your golden light!
   She sleeps! . . .
That was the first sound in the song of love!
 Scarce more than silence is, and yet a sound.
         The Spanish Student

31. Between the dark and the daylight,
   When the night is beginning to lower,
 Comes a pause in the day's occupations,
   That is known as the Children's Hour.
         The Children's Hour

32. The day is done, and the darkness
   Falls from the wings of Night,
 As a feather is wafted downward
   From an eagle in his flight

    . . . .

A feeling of sadness and longing
   That is not akin to pain,
And resembles sorrow only
   As the mist resembles the rain.

    . . . .

And the night shall be filled with music,
  And the cares that infest the day,
Shall fold their tents, like the Arabs,
  And as silently steal away.

"The Day is Done"

33. I shot an arrow into the air,
  It fell to earth, I knew not where.

The Arrow and the Song

34. Though the mills of God grind slowly,
  yet they grind exceeding small;
Though with patience he stands waiting,
  with exactness grinds he all.

Retribution

35. This is the forest primeval

. . . .

Silently one by one, in the infinite meadows of heaven
Blossomed the lovely stars, the forget-me-nots of the
  angels.
Talk not of wasted affection! affection never was wasted;
  If it enrich not the heart of another, its waters,
    returning
Back to their springs, like the rain, shall fill them full of
  refreshment:
  That which the fountain sends forth returns again to
    the fountain.

. . . .

Then from the neighboring thicket, the mocking-bird,
  wildest of singers,
  Swinging aloft on a willow spray that hung over
    the water,
Shook from his little throat such floods of delicious music
  That the whole air and the woods and the waves
    seemed silent to listen

. . . .

This is the compass-flower, that the finger of God has
  planted

Here in the houseless wild, to direct the traveller's
    journey
Over the sea-like, pathless, limitless waste of the desert.
Evangeline

36. Thou, too, sail on, O Ship of State!
Sail on, O Union, strong and great!
Humanity with all its fears,
With all the hopes of future years,
Is hanging breathless on thy fate!

.   .   .   .

Our hearts, our hopes, are all with thee,
Our hearts, our hopes, our prayers, our tears,
Our faith triumphant o'er our fears,
Are all with thee,—are all with thee!

.   .   .   .

It is the heart and not the brain
That to the highest doth attain,
And he who followeth Love's behest
Far excelleth all the rest.
The Building of the Ship

37. Nothing useless is, or low;
    Each thing in its place is best;
And what seems but idle show
    Strengthens and supports the rest.
The Builders

38. All your strength if in your union
All your danger is in discord;
Therefore be at peace henceforward,
And as brothers live together.

.   .   .   .

As unto the bow the cord is,
So unto the man is woman,
Though she bends him, she obeys him,
Though she draws him, yet she follows;
Useless each without the other!

.   .   .   .

Love is sunshine, hate is shadow,
Life is checkered shade and sunshine.

The Song of Hiawatha

39. Why don't you speak for yourself, John?

The Courtship of Miles Standish

40. A Lady with a Lamp shall stand
In the great history of the land,
A noble type of good,
Heroic womanhood.

Santa Filomena

41. Listen, my children, and you shall hear
Of the midnight ride of Paul Revere.

.   .   .   .

One if by land, and two if by sea;
And I on the opposite shore will be.

.   .   .   .

The fate of a nation was riding that night.

.   .   .   .

A voice in the darkness, a knock at the door,
And a voice that shall echo forevermore!

Tales of a Wayside Inn: Paul Revere's Ride

42. Ships that pass in the night, and speak each other in
passing,
Only a signal shown, and a distant voice in the darkness;
So on the ocean of life we pass and speak one another,
Only a look and a voice; then darkness again and a silence.

Tales of a Wayside Inn: Elizabeth

43. "O Caesar, we who are about to die
Salute you!" was the gladiators' cry
In the arena, standing face to face
With death and with the Roman populace.

.   .   .   .

Let him not boast who puts his armor on
As he who puts it off, the battle done.

.   .   .   .

Write on your doors the saying wise and bold,
"Be bold! be bold!" and everywhere
 —"Be bold;
Be not too bold!"

. . . .

Better like Hector in the field to die,
Than like a perfumed Paris turn and fly.

. . . .

Ye, against whose familiar names not yet
The fatal asterisk of death is set.

. . . .

The love of learning, the sequestered nooks,
And all the sweet serenity of books.

. . . .

Ah, nothing is too late,
Till the tired heart shall cease to palpitate.
Cato learned Greek at eighty; Sophocles
Wrote his grand *Oedipus,* and Simonides
Bore off the prize of verse from his compeers,
When each had numbered more than fourscore years.

. . . .

Chaucer, at Woodstock with the nightingales,
At sixty, wrote the *Canterbury Tales;*
Goethe at Weimar, toiling to the last,
Composed *Faust* when eighty years were past.

. . . .

For age is opportunity no less
Than youth itself, though in another dress,
And as the evening twilight fades away
The sky is filled with stars, invisible by day.

        Morituri Salutamus

44. She knew the life-long martyrdom,
   The weariness, the endless pain
 Of waiting for some one to come
   Who nevermore would come again.

        Vittoria Colonna

45. Not in the clamor of the crowded street,
   Not in the shouts and plaudits of the throng,
  But in ourselves, are triumph and defeat.

               The Poets

46. The holiest of all holidays are those
  Kept by ourselves in silence and apart;
  The secret anniversaries of the heart.

               Holidays

47. Go forth to meet the shadowy
  Future without fear and with a manly heart.

    ·   ·   ·   ·

O, there is nothing holier, in this life of ours, than the first consciousness of love,—the first fluttering of its silken wings.

    ·   ·   ·   ·

  Nature is a revelation of God;
  Art a revelation of man.

               Hyperion

48. There was a little girl
  And she had a little curl
  Right in the middle of her forehead;
  And when she was good
  She was very, very good,
  But when she was bad she was horrid.

         There Was a Little Girl

49. Midnight! The outpost of advancing day!
  The frontier town and citadel of night!

              Two Rivers

50. For some must follow and some command,
  Though all are made of clay!

               Kéramos

51. Stay, stay at home, my heart, and rest;
  Home-keeping hearts are happiest,
  For those that wander they know not where
  Are full of trouble and full of care;
  To stay at home is best.

               Song

52. At first laying down, as a fact fundamental,
    That nothing with God can be accidental.

Christus

53. I heard the bells on Christmas Day
    Their old familiar carols play,
    And wild and sweet
    The words repeat
    Of Peace on earth, good-will to men!

Christmas Bells

54. *Emigravit,* is the inscription on the tombstone where he
    lies;
    Dead he is not, but departed—for the artist never dies.

Nuremberg

55. I stood on the bridge at midnight,
    As the clocks were striking the hour,
    And the moon rose over the city,
    Behind the dark church tower.

The Bridge

JOHN GREENLEAF WHITTIER
(1807–1892)

A Quaker, born near Haverhill, Massachusetts, the scantily educated Whittier achieved a popularity rivalled only by Longfellow's, despite their greatly differing backgrounds. In fact, though Whittier published poems in his youth, he early diverted his talents to writing, speaking and political activity in favor of abolition of slavery, working closely with Garrison, until about 1840. At that time ill health [he lived another 52 years] caused him to retreat to the quieter life of belles-lettres. By 1857 he was so well known that the *Atlantic Monthly* invited him like the elder Holmes to become a contributor.

1. Art's perfect forms no moral need,
   And beauty is its own excuse;
   But for the dull and flowerless weed
   Some healing virtue still must plead.

Songs of Labor

2. Heap high the farmer's wintry hoard!
    Heap high the golden corn!
No richer gift has Autumn poured
    From out her lavish horn!

The Corn-Song

3. When faith is lost, when honor dies,
    The man is dead!

Ichabod

4. "Shoot if you must, this old gray head,
    But spare your country's flag," she said.

Barbara Frietchie

5. Yet sometimes glimpses on my sight,
Through present wrong the eternal right;
And, step by step, since time began,
I see the steady gain of man.

The Chapel of the Hermits

6. Blessings on thee, little man,
Barefoot boy, with cheek of tan!

. . . .

Health that mocks the doctor's rules,
Knowledge never learned of schools, . . .

The Barefoot Boy

7. We cross the prairie as of old
    The pilgrims crossed the sea,
To make the West, as they the East,
    The homestead of the free!

The Kansas Emigrants

8. For of all sad words of tongue or pen,
The saddest are these: "It might have been!"

Maud Muller

9. The windows of my soul I throw
    Wide open to the sun. . . .

. . . .

No longer forward nor behind
    I look in hope or fear;
But, grateful, take the good I find,

The best of now and here.

My Psalm

10. Heaven's gate is shut to him who comes alone;
    Save thou a soul, and it shall save thy own.

The Two Rabbis

11. And close at hand the basket stood
    With nuts from brown October's wood.

Snow-Bound

12. What moistens the lips and what brightens the eye?
    What calls back the past, like the rich pumpkin pie?

    .   .   .   .

    O,—fruit beloved of boyhood!—the old days recalling,
    When wood-grapes were purpling and brown nuts were
        falling,
    When wild, ugly faces we carved in its skin,
    Glaring out through the dark with a candle within!

The Pumpkin

13. Again the blackbirds sing; the streams
        Wake, laughing, from their winter dreams,
    And tremble in the April showers
        The tassels of the maple flowers.

The Singer

14. So let it be in God's own might
    We gird us for the coming fight,
    And strong in him whose cause is ours
    In conflict with unholy powers,
    We grasp the weapons he has given,—
    The Light, the Truth, and Love of Heaven.

The Moral Warfare

SAMUEL FRANCIS SMITH
(1808–1895)

A Baptist clergyman and poet, very properly Boston born and Harvard educated, completed his postgraduate work at Andover Theological Seminary. Smith wrote many hymns, but he would have slipped anonymously into the honorable past, except for one verse which he composed while still at Andover, 1831.

> My country, 'tis of thee,
> Sweet land of liberty,
>   Of thee I sing:
> Land where my fathers died,
> Land of the pilgrims' pride,
> From every mountain-side
>   Let freedom ring.

> .   .   .   .

> Our fathers' God, to thee,
> Author of liberty,
>   To thee I sing;
> Long may our land be bright
> With freedom's holy light;
> Protect us by Thy might,
>   Great God, our King!

America

PARK BENJAMIN (1809–1864)

BENJAMIN divided a rather brief literary career in New York, to which he came from his birthplace, British Guiana, between editing several magazines, sensational reportage and the writing of verse that was largely mediocre. From the occasionally memorable latter came one bit that promises to live long among quotations.

> I'm King of the Dead, and I make my throne
> On a monument slab of marble cold—
> And my scepter of rule is the spade I hold.
> Come they from cottage or come they from hall,
> Mankind are my subjects, all, all, all!
> Let them loiter in pleasure, or toilfully spin,
> I gather them in—I gather them in.

The Old Sexton

OLIVER WENDELL HOLMES, SR. (1809–1894)

OLIVER Wendell Holmes? We might very well ask, "Which one?" The elder Holmes, while a twenty-one year old law student at Harvard, attracted national attention with his poem "Old Ironsides." Switching to medicine in 1831, he studied both at Harvard and in Paris. As a doctor teaching anatomy and physiology at Dartmouth and Harvard he found time to establish the Tremont Medical School in Boston in 1838. The wit that sparked his scientific lectures won him invitations for literary lectures as well on the lyceum circuit. These in turn brought him great popularity. By 1857, well established as a poet and essayist, he became a regular contributor to The *Atlantic Monthly*, which he named. His contributions to the *Atlantic* were collected, over a span of years, into the lively "Breakfast-Table" series.

1. Every event that a man would master must be mounted on the run, and no man ever caught the reins of a thought except as it galloped past him.

2. A goose flies by a chart which the Royal Geographical Society could not improve.

3. Sin has many tools, but a lie is the handle which fits them all.

4. I firmly believe that if the whole *materia medica* as now used could be sunk to the bottom of the sea, it would be all the better for mankind—and all the worse for the fishes.

Address to Massachusetts Medical Society, May 30, 1860

5. Vulgar people can't be still.

6. The world's great men have not commonly been great scholars, nor its great scholars great men.

7. The world is always ready to receive talent with open arms.

8. Why can't somebody give us a list of things everybody thinks and nobody says, and another list of things that everybody says and nobody thinks?

9. Man has his will,—but woman has her way.

10. Apology is only egotism wrong side out.

11. What a blessed thing it is that nature, when she invented, manufactured and patented her authors, contrived to make critics out of the chips that were left!

12. Boston State-house is the hub of the solar system. You couldn't pry that out of a Boston man if you had the tire of all creation straightened out for a crow-bar.

13. Fashion is only the attempt to realize art in living forms and social intercourse.

14. A man must *get* a thing before he can *forget* it.

15. The brain is the palest of all the internal organs and the heart the reddest. Whatever comes from the brain carries the hue of the place it came from, and whatever comes from the heart carries the heat and color of its birthplace.

16. He comes from the Brahmin caste of New England. This is the harmless, inoffensive, untitled aristocracy.

17. Everybody likes and respects self-made men. It is a great deal better to be made in that way than not to be made at all.

18. Insanity is often the logic of an accurate mind overtaxed.

19. Put not your trust in money, but put your money in trust.

20. There is that glorious epicurean paradox uttered by my friend the historian [John Lothrop Motley], in one of his flashing moments: "Give us the luxuries of life, and we will dispense with its necessaries." To this must certainly be added that other saying of one of the wittiest of men [Thomas Gold Appleton]: "Good Americans, when they die, go to Paris."

21. The axis of the earth sticks out visibly through the centre of each and every town or city.

22. Knowledge and timber shouldn't be much used till they are seasoned.

23. To be seventy years young is sometimes far more cheerful and hopeful than to be forty years old.

On the Seventieth Birthday of Julia Ward Howe, May 27, 1889

24. Soft is the breath of a maiden's yes:
   Not the light gossamer stirs with less;
   But never a cable that holds so fast
   Through all the battles of war and blast.

Songs of Many Seasons

25. Day hath put on his jacket, and around
His burning bosom buttoned it with stars.

Evening

26. Youth fades; love drops, the leaves of friendship fall;
A mother's secret hope outlives them all.

A Mother's Secret

27. Ay, tear her tattered ensign down!
Long has it waved on high,
And many an eye has danced to see
That banner in the sky.

. . . .

Nail to the mast her holy flag,
Set every threadbare sail,
And give her to the god of storms,
The lightning and the gale!

Old Ironsides

28. The mossy marbles rest
On the lips that he has pressed
In their bloom,
And the names he loved to hear
Have been carved for many a year
On the tomb.

. . . .

I know it is a sin
For me to sit and grin
At him here;
But the old three-cornered hat,
And the breeches, and all that,
Are so queer!

. . . .

And if I should live to be
The last leaf upon the tree
In the spring,
Let them smile, as I do now,
At the old forsaken bough
Where I cling.

The Last Leaf

29. Little I ask; my wants are few;
    I only wish a hut of stone,
    (A *very plain* brown stone will do,)
    That I may call my own;—

                                                        Contentment

30. Age, like distance, lends a double charm.

                  .   .   .   .

    Wear seemly gloves; not black, nor yet too light,
    And least of all the pair that once was white.

                                          A Rhymed Lesson

31. Learn the sweet magic of a cheerful face;
    Not always smiling, but at least serene.

                                          The Morning Visit

32. Wake in our breast the living fires,
    The holy faith that warmed our sires;
    Thy hand hath made our Nation free;
    To die for her is serving Thee.

                                                        Army Hymn

33. I love to hear thine earnest voice,
        Wherever thou art hid. . . .
    Thou say'st an undisputed thing
        In such a solemn way.

                                                        To an Insect

34. We will not speaks of years tonight,—
        For what have years to bring
    But larger floods of love and light
        And sweeter songs to sing?

                          On James Russell Lowell's Birthday

35. Oh for one hour of youthful joy!
        Give me back my twentieth spring!

                                          The Old Man Dreams

36. One flag, one land, one head, one hand,
        One Nation, evermore!

                          Voyage of the Good Ship Union

37. Build thee more stately mansions, O my soul,
        As the swift seasons roll!
    Leave thy low-vaulted past!

Let each new temple, nobler than the last,
Shut thee from heaven with a dome more vast,
    Till thou at length art free,
Leaving thine outgrown shell by life's unresting sea!

The Chambered Nautilus

38. Our truest steps are human still,—
To walk unswerving were divine.

The Crooked Footpath

39. There is no time like the old time, when you and I were
young.

No Time Like the Old Time

40. Have you heard of the wonderful one-hoss shay,
That was built in such a logical way
It ran a hundred years to a day?

.   .   .   .

A general flavor of mild decay.

.   .   .   .

Logic is logic, that's all I say.

.   .   .   .

It went to pieces all at once,—
All at once, and nothing first,
Just as bubbles do when they burst.

The Deacon's Masterpiece

41. Learn to give
Money to colleges while you live.
Don't be silly and think you'll try
To bother the colleges, when you die,
With codicil this, and codicil that,
That Knowledge may starve while Law grows fat;
For there never was pitcher that wouldn't spill,
And there's always a flaw in a donkey's will.

Parson Turell's Legacy

42. Where we love is home,
Home that our feet may leave, but not our hearts.

Homesick in Heaven

43. I come not here your morning hour to sadden,
    A limping pilgrim, leaning on his staff,—
I, who have never deemed it sin to gladden
    This vale of sorrows with a wholesome laugh.

The Iron Gate

ABRAHAM LINCOLN (1809–1865)

AS with George Washington, it would be sheer presumption to attempt in a paragraph a portrait of Lincoln's life. His memorable statements are relatively brief, compared to those of professional writers or lecturers; in fact, he seemed to have little sense of his own historical significance, which indicates the character of his humility. For instance, his Gettysburg Address [one of the world's great documents] was spoken from notes. Only afterward was the speech put in written form, by news correspondents who compared their notes and checked them with Lincoln on the train ride back to Washington. These same correspondents gave the main report of that day at Gettysburg to Edward Everett, the official "orator," whose memorized speech was also made available in text.

1. I go for all sharing the privileges of the government who assist in bearing its burdens. *Letter, 1836*

2. There is no grievance that is a fit object of redress by mob law. *Speech, 1837*

3. The ballot is stronger than the bullet. *Speech, 1856*

4. I believe that this government cannot endure permanently half slave and half free.

Speech, Illinois Republican Convention, 1858

5. As I would not be a slave, so I would not be a master. This expresses my idea of democracy. Whatever differs from this, to the extent of the difference, is no democracy. *Letter, 1858*

6. If we do not make common cause to save the good ship of the Union on this voyage, nobody will have a chance to pilot her on another voyage. *Speech, 1861*

7. This country, with its institutions, belongs to the people who inhabit it. . . . Why should there not be a patient confidence

in the ultimate justice of the people? Is there any better or equal hope in the world?

You can have no oath registered in heaven to destroy the Government; while I shall have the most solemn one to "preserve, protect, and defend" it. . . .

No government proper ever had a provision in its organic law for its own termination. . . .

While the people retain their virtue and vigilance, no administration, by any extreme of wickedness or folly, can very seriously injure the government in the short space of four years.

First Inaugural Address, 1861

8. My paramount object in this struggle is to save the Union, and is not either to save or destroy slavery. If I could save the Union without freeing any slave, I would do it; and if I could do it by freeing all the slaves, I would do it; and if I could save it by freeing some and leaving others alone, I would also do that.

Letter, 1862

9. Fourscore and seven years ago our fathers brought forth on this continent a new nation, conceived in liberty and dedicated to the proposition that all men are created equal. Now we are engaged in a great civil war, testing whether that nation, or any nation so conceived and so dedicated, can long endure. We are met on a great battlefield of that war. We have come to dedicate a portion of that field as a final resting-place for those who here gave their lives that that nation might live. It is altogether fitting and proper that we should do this. But, in a larger sense, we cannot dedicate, we cannot consecrate, we cannot hallow this ground. The brave men, living and dead, who struggled here have consecrated it far above our poor power to add or to detract. The world will little note nor long remember what we say here, but it can never forget what they did here. It is for us, the living, rather to be dedicated here to the unfinished work which they who fought here have thus far nobly so advanced. It is rather for us to be here dedicated to the great task remaining before us—that from these honored dead we take increased devotion to that cause for which they gave the last full measure of devotion; that we here highly resolve that these dead shall not have died in vain; that this nation,

under God, shall have a new birth of freedom; and that government of the people, by the people, for the people shall not perish from the earth.

Gettysburg Address, 1863

10. I desire so to conduct the affairs of this Administration that if at the end, when I come to lay down the reins of power, I have lost every other friend on earth, I shall have at least one friend left, and that friend shall be down inside of me.

To Missouri Committee of Seventy, 1864

11. I have not permitted myself to suppose that either the convention or the league have concluded that I am either the greatest or the best man in the country, but rather they have concluded that it is not best to swap horses while crossing the river, and have further concluded that I am not so poor a horse that they might not make a botch of it in trying to swap.

To National Union League, 1864

12. With malice toward none, with charity for all, with firmness in the right as God gives us to see the right, let us finish the work we are in, to bind up the nation's wounds, to care for him who shall have borne the battle, and for his widow and for his orphans, to do all which may achieve and cherish a just and lasting peace among ourselves and with all nations.

Second Inaugural Address, 1865

EDGAR ALLAN POE (1809–1849)

THE words "haunting melancholy" have rightly been used to describe the underlying motif of Poe's writings which, in his brief and chaotic life, ranged over the field of the short story (of which he was the master), essays, articles, literary criticism and poetry. Upon all of these literary forms he left his special mark. One wonders what he might have achieved if the compulsive alcoholism from which he suffered had not cut short his career.

1. The world is a great ocean upon which we encounter more tempestuous storms than calms.

2. It is with literature as with law and empire—an estab-

lished name is an estate in tenure, or a throne in possession.

3. The Romans worshipped their standard; and the Roman standard happened to be an eagle. Our standard is only one tenth of an eagle,—a dollar,—but we make all even by adoring it with tenfold devotion.

4. With me poetry has been not a purpose, but a passion; and the passions should be held in reverence; they must not—they can not at will be excited, with an eye to the paltry compensations, or the more paltry commendations, of mankind.

5. I would define, in brief, the Poetry of words as the Rythmical Creation of Beauty. Its sole arbiter is Taste.

6. *Glitter*—and in that one word how much of all that is detestable do we express!

7. Perverseness is one of the primitive impulses of the human heart.

8. There are chords in the hearts of the most reckless which can not be touched without emotion. Even with the utterly lost, to whom life and death are equally jests, there are matters of which no jest can be made.

9. The boundaries which divide Life from Death are at best shadowy and vague. Who shall say where the one ends, and where the other begins?

10. Those who dream by day are cognizant of many things which escape those who dream only by night.

11. All that we see or seem
    Is but a dream within a dream.
                    A Dream Within a Dream

12. Vastness! and Age! and Memories of Eld!
    Silence! and Desolation! and dim Night!
                    The Coliseum

13. This maiden she lived with no other thought
    Than to love and be loved by me.

            .   .   .   .

    I was a child and she was a child,
        In this kingdom by the sea;
    But we loved with a love that was more than love—
        I and my Annabel Lee;

With a love that the winged seraphs of heaven
　　Coveted her and me.

Annabel Lee

14. Hear the sledges with the bells,
　　　Silver bells!
　What a world of merriment their melody foretells!
　How they tinkle, tinkle, tinkle
　　In the icy air of night!
　While the stars that over-sprinkle
　　All the heavens seem to tinkle
　With a crystalline delight
　　Keeping time, time, time
　In a sort of Runic rhyme
　　To the tintinnabulation that so musically wells
　From the bells, bells, bells, bells,
　　Bells, bells, bells—
　From the jingling and the tinkling of the bells.
　Hear the mellow wedding bells,
　　Golden bells!
　What a world of happiness their harmony foretells!
　　Through the balmy air of night
　　How they ring out their delight!

The Bells

15. Come! Let the burial rite be read—
　　The funeral song be sung!—
　A dirge for her, the doubly dead
　　In that she died so young.

Lenore

16. Once upon a midnight dreary, while I pondered, weak
　　　and weary,
　Over many a quaint and curious volume of forgotten
　　　lore,—
　While I nodded, nearly napping, suddenly there came a
　　　tapping,
　As of someone gently rapping,

　　　　　.　　.　　.　　.

Ah, distinctly I remember, it was in the bleak December,
And each separate dying ember wrought its ghost upon
the floor.

. . . .

Deep into that darkness peering, long I stood there,
wondering, fearing,
Doubting, dreaming dreams no mortal ever dared to
dream before;

. . . .

[the Raven]
Perched upon a bust of Pallas just above my chamber
door:
Perched, and sat, and nothing more.

. . . .

Quoth the Raven, "Nevermore."

. . . .

And the Raven, never flitting, still is sitting, still is sitting,
On the pallid bust of Pallas just above my chamber door;
And his eyes have all the seeming of a demon's that is
dreaming,
And the lamp-light o'er him streaming throws his shadow
on the floor,
And my soul from out that shadow that lies floating on
the floor,
Shall be lifted—nevermore!

The Raven

17. Helen, thy beauty is to me
        Like those Nicaean barks of yore,
    That gently, o'er a perfumed sea,
        The weary, wayworn wanderer bore
        To his own native shore.

. . . .

To the glory that was Greece,
And the grandeur that was Rome.

To Helen

PHINEAS T. BARNUM (1810–1891)

IN the history of showmen and showmanship, Barnum was the first to concede his own pre-eminence, writing and re-writing the story of his triumphs in an autobiography first published in 1855, and brought up to date every few years until his death.

There's a sucker born every minute.

(SARAH) MARGARET FULLER (1810–1850)

THESE selected quotations from the writings of this Boston woman hint at her importance in the literary world (she was a first-rate newspaper woman) and in the feminist movement, but give no clue to the romance of her own life—as a noted translator of German works, a leader of the transcendentalist movement, as the bride in 1847 of Mazzini's disciple, the Marchese Ossoli, alongside whom she fought in the Italian revolution of 1848–49. She finally drowned with her husband and baby, off Fire Island, on a homeward voyage in 1850.

1. Women could take part in the processions, the songs, the dances, of old religions; no one fancied their delicacy was impaired by appearing in public for such a cause.

2. In order that she may be able to give her hand with dignity, she [woman] must be able to stand alone.

3. It does not follow because many books are written by persons in America that there exists an American literature. Books which imitate or represent the thoughts and life of Europe do not constitute an American literature. Before such can exist, an original idea must animate this nation and fresh currents of life must call into life such fresh thoughts along its shores.

4. . . . as the principle of liberty is better understood, . . . a broader protest is made on behalf of women.

JAMES SLOAN GIBBONS
(1810–1892)

WHEN the Civil War began, President Lincoln called originally upon the northern States to supply 75,000 soldiers. It quickly became apparent, however, that the war would be on a much greater scale, so he called for an additional 300,000. [The conscription was later to swell to millions.] This second call prompted this banker, abolitionist, author, soldier and citizen to write a catchy tune etched with pathos that won it a place in America's library of famous songs.

> We are coming, Father Abraham, three hundred thousand
>   more,
> From Mississippi's winding stream and from New England's shore;
> We leave our ploughs and workshops, our wives and children dear,
> With hearts too full for utterance, with but a single tear.
>
> *We Are Coming, Father Abraham*

THEODORE PARKER (1810–1860)

THIS theologian and social reformer, born at Lexington, Massachusetts possessed a formidable intellect that enabled him—self-taught—to pass Harvard's graduation examination without ever attending classes and to enter directly Harvard Divinity School, from which he was graduated at the age of twenty-six years. First a preacher, his skill as an orator brought him popularity on the lyceum circuit where he declaimed on the issues of antislavery and prison-reform. He also composed hymns.

1. Truth never yet fell dead in the streets; it has such affinity with the soul of man, the seed however broadcast will catch somewhere and produce its hundredfold.

2. Man never falls so low that he can see nothing higher than himself.

3. All men desire to be immortal.

4. A democracy,—that is a government of all the people, by all the people, for all the people; of course, a government of the principles of eternal justice, the unchanging law of God; for shortness' sake, I will call it the idea of Freedom.

5. We look to Thee; the truth is still the Light
      Which guides the nations, groping on their way,
   Stumbling and falling in disastrous night,
      Yet hoping ever for the perfect day.

The Way, the Truth, and the Life

HORACE GREELEY (1811–1872)

IN 1841, Greeley established the *New York Tribune* which in the thirty years under his editorship became the prototype of modern newspapers—known for its outspoken editorials, expert handling of the broad range of news and encouragement of leading writers. An exponent of unionism Greeley helped his own printers to organize; he not only preached profit-sharing, he put it into practice at the *Tribune*. Capping all of these accomplishments was his advocacy of western settlement, to which he gave considerable editorial backing.

1. Go west, young man, and grow up with the country.

2. Common sense is very uncommon.

3. Talent without tact is only half talent.

4. The illusion that times that were are better than those that are, has probably pervaded all ages.

5. Wisdom is never dear, provided the article is genuine.

6. If, on a full and final review, my life and practice shall be found unworthy of my principles, let due infamy be heaped on my memory; but let none be led thereby to distrust the principles to which I proved recreant, nor yet the ability of some to adorn them by a suitable life and conversation. To unerring time be all this committed.

WENDELL PHILLIPS (1811–1884)

THIS "proper Bostonian" in every respect, wealthy and brilliant, graduated both from Harvard College and Harvard Law School, and thereafter devoted himself to fights for "causes" from abolition to pro-hibition, labor's rights and currency reform. In his long career as writer and lecturer, he built a reputation as an orator comparable to those of the giants Edward Everett and Daniel Webster.

1. Exigencies create the necessary abilities to meet and conquer them.

2. Revolutions are not made; they come.

3. Christianity is a battle, not a dream.

4. Physical bravery is an animal instinct; moral bravery is a much higher and truer courage.

5. What is defeat? Nothing but education, nothing but the first step to something better.

6. Every man meets his Waterloo at last.

7. What is fanaticism today is the fashionable creed tomorrow, and trite as the multiplication table a week later.

8. One, on God's side, is a majority.

9. Governments exist to protect the rights of minorities. The loved and the rich need no protection,—they have many friends and few enemies.

10. Health lies in labor, and there is no royal road to it but through toil.

11. Hearts are stronger than swords.

12. We live under a government of men and morning newspapers. . . . Let me make the newspapers, and I care not what is preached in the pulpit or what is enacted in Congress.

13. Take the whole range of imaginative literature, and we are all wholesale borrowers. In every matter that relates to invention, to use, or beauty or form, we are borrowers.

14. Great political questions stir the deepest nature of one-half the nation; but they pass far above and over the heads of the other half.

15. Power is ever stealing from the many to the few.

16. As the Greek said, "Many men know how to flatter, few men know how to praise."

17. The keener the want, the lustier the growth.

HARRIET BEECHER STOWE (1811–1896)

A brilliant woman, ardently interested in reform movements such as prohibition and woman suffrage, the author of *Uncle Tom's Cabin; or, Life Among the Lowly,* though she hated slavery was not an abolitionist. She considered her contemporaries in that field too extreme. She wrote the best-seller of the nineteenth century while bringing up a family of six children on very meager resources. She was a prolific writer of novels and religious poems; one hymn "Still, Still with Thee" is still a universal favorite.

1. I 'spect I growed. Don't think nobody never made me.

. . . .

I's wicked—I is. I's mighty wicked, anyhow.

Topsy in Uncle Tom's Cabin

2. Still, still with Thee, when purple morning breaketh,
   When the bird waketh and the shadows flee.

Still, Still with Thee

CHARLES SUMNER (1811–1874)

THIS senator from Massachusetts (1851–74) was one of the large corps of Boston-Harvard lawyers successful in politics. A famous orator, he was unmerciful and vindictive in debate. As a chief architect of the misnamed Reconstruction Program under which the vanquished South was literally ruined, he contributed to a shameful chapter in American history. All this should be kept in mind when we read his eloquent expression of the highest sentiments.

1. There is the national flag. He must be cold, indeed, who can look upon its folds rippling in the breeze without pride of country. If in a foreign land, the flag is companionship, and country itself with all its endearments. . . . White is for purity; red, for valor; blue, for justice. And altogether, bunting, stripes, stars, and colors, blazing in the sky, make the flag of our country, to be cherished by all our hearts, to be upheld by all our hands.

2. No true and permanent Fame can be founded except in labors which promote the happiness of mankind.

3. The age of chivalry has gone; the age of humanity has come.

4. Let the bugles sound the *Truce of God* to the whole world forever.

5. There are two sorts of pity; one is a balm and the other a poison; the first is realized by our friends, the last by our enemies.

6. Where Slavery is there Liberty cannot be; and where Liberty is there Slavery cannot be.

HENRY WARD BEECHER (1813–1887)

LIKE his sister Harriet Beecher Stowe, this clergyman was an advocate of abolition and woman suffrage; he was an equally vociferous supporter of the theory of evolution. He had few competitors in the field of the popular lecture, for his knowledge and imagination were vast and he had a wonderful gift for turning a phrase.

1. Fear secretes acids; but love and trust are sweet juices.

2. Coming to [the Bible] through commentaries is much like looking at a landscape through garret windows, over which generations of unmolested spiders have spun their webs.

3. Many men build as cathedrals were built, the part nearest the ground finished; but the parts which soar toward heaven, the turrets and the spires, forever incomplete.

4. Every charitable act is a stepping stone toward heaven.

5. Conceited men often seem a harmless kind of men, who,

by an overweening self-respect, relieve others of the duty of respecting them at all.

6. A conservative young man has wound up his life before it was unreeled. We expect old men to be conservative; but when a nation's young men are so, its funeral bell is already rung.

7. The cynic is one who never sees a good quality in a man, and never fails to see a bad one. He is the human owl, vigilant in darkness and blind to light, mousing for vermin, and never seeing noble game. The cynic puts all human actions into two classes—openly bad and secretly bad.

8. A church debt is the devil's salary.

9. It is defeat that turns bone to flint; it is defeat that turns gristle to muscle; it is defeat that makes men invincible.

10. Doctrine is nothing but the skin of truth set up and stuffed.

11. In things pertaining to enthusiasm no man is sane who does not know how to be insane on proper occasions.

12. There is no such thing as white lies; a lie is as black as a coalpit, and twice as foul.

13. God planted fear in the soul as truly as he planted hope and courage. Fear is a kind of bell, or gong, which rings the mind into quick life and avoidance upon the approach of danger. It is the soul's signal for rallying.

14. Flowers may beckon towards us, but they speak toward heaven and God.

15. Flowers have an expression of countenance as much as men or animals. Some seem to smile; some have a sad expression; some are pensive and diffident; others again are plain, honest, and upright, like the broad-faced sunflower and the hollyhock.

16. God pardons like a mother, who kisses the offense into everlasting forgetfulness.

17. Good-humor makes all things tolerable.

18. We get to the grave of a friend saying, "A man is dead," but angels throng about him saying, "A man is born."

19. Heaven will be inherited by every man who has heaven in his soul.

20. A tool is but the extension of a man's hand, and a machine is but a complex tool. And he that invents a machine augments the power of a man and the well-being of mankind.

21. When God thought of mother, He must have laughed with satisfaction, and framed it quickly—so rich, so deep, so divine, so full of soul, power, and beauty, was the conception.

22. Private opinion is weak, but public opinion is almost omnipotent.

23. There is no friendship, no love, like that of the parent for the child.

24. The philosophy of one century is the common sense of the next.

25. Men must read for amusement as well as for knowledge.

26. In this world, it is not what we take up, but what we give up, that makes us rich.

27. Success is full of promise till men get it; and then it is last year's nest, from which the bird has flown.

28. Victories that are cheap are cheap. Those only are worth having which come as the result of hard fighting.

29. The world is God's workshop for making men in.

CHRISTOPHER PEARSE CRANCH (1813–1892)

PAINTER Cranch, one of the first of Americans to break away from sectionalism, was born in Alexandria, Virginia, a graduate of Columbian College in Washington and of Harvard Divinity School. He preached, painted and wrote without regional partiality.

1. Thought is deeper than all speech,
    Feeling deeper than all thought;
  Souls to souls can never teach
    What unto themselves was taught.

Thought

2. One day in the bluest of summer weather,
    Sketching under a whispering Oak,
  I heard five bobolinks laughing together,
    Over some ornithological joke.

The Bobolink

JESSE HUTCHINSON, JR. (1813–1853)

THIS popular singer-composer never made the lists of "greats" of his day, but his doggerel verses and jaunty melodies marked the beginnings of popular songs which interpreted the American theme.

1. Of all the mighty nations
      In the east or in the west,
   O this glorious Yankee nation
      Is the greatest and the best.
   We have room for all creation,
      And our banner is unfurled,
   Here's a general invitation
      To the people of the world.

   Refrain

   Uncle Sam is rich enough to give us all a farm.
   Uncle Sam's Farm

2. Then, ho, brothers, ho
   To California we go;
   There's plenty of gold in the world we're told
   On the banks of the Sacramento.

   Ho for California

CHARLOTTE CUSHMAN (1816–1876)

THIS Boston-born actress made her debut as an opera singer, but loss of her singing voice turned her to drama, where she displayed an extraordinary talent in playing both female and male Shakespearian roles, including Romeo and Hamlet. Her gift for original expression, though less well known, was equally appreciated by her contemporaries.

1. Goethe said there would be little left of him if he were to discard what he owed to others.

2. God conceived the world, that was poetry; He formed it, that was sculpture; He colored it, that was painting; He peopled it with living beings, that was the grand, divine, eternal drama.

JOHN GODFREY SAXE (1816–1887)

AS the occupations of novelist and lecturer began to come into their own in American life in the first half of the nineteenth century, so did that of the popular poet. The modern troubador won a ready audience; his work was not as ambitious as his more serious forbears, but he owed much to their inspirations. Saxe, editor of the Burlington, Vermont *Sentinel,* was one of these popular poets. He built a national reputation through publication in *Harper's* and other leading periodicals, and through collections of his own works.

1. There's a castle in Spain, very charming to see,
        Though built without money or toil;
    Of this handsome estate I am owner in fee,
        And paramount lord of the soil.

    My Castle in Spain

2. The saying is wise, though it sounds like a jest,
        That the "gods allow us to be in their debt,"
    For though we may think we are specially blest,
        We are certain to pay for the favors we get!

    . . . .

    Old Care has a mortgage on every estate,
    And that's what you pay for the wealth that you get.

    Gift of the Gods

3. When skies are clear, expect the cloud;
        In darkness, wait the coming light;
    Whatever be thy fate to-day,
        Remember, "This will pass away!"

    The Old Man's Motto

4. Of all amusements for the mind,
        From logic down to fishing,

There isn't one that you can find
So very cheap as "wishing."

.   .   .   .

I wish that practising was not
So different from preaching.

Wishing

5. I'm growing fonder of my staff;
I'm growing dimmer in the eyes;
I'm growing fainter in my laugh;
I'm growing deeper in my sighs;
I'm growing careless of my dress;
I'm growing frugal of my gold;
I'm growing wise; I'm growing—yes,—
I'm growing old!

I'm Growing Old

6. Of all the notable things on earth,
The queerest one is pride of birth,
Among our "fierce Democracie!"
A bridge across a hundred years,
Without a prop to save it from sneers,—
Not even a couple of rotten Peers,—
A thing for laughter, fleers, and jeers,
Is American aristocracy.

.   .   .   .

Depend upon it, my snobbish friend,
Your family thread you can't ascend,
Without good reason to apprehend
You may find it waxed at the farther end
By some plebeian vocation;
Or, worse than that, your boasted Line
May end in a loop of stronger twine,
That plagued some worthy relation.

The Proud Miss MacBride

7. He says a thousand pleasant things,—
But never says, "Adieu."

My Familiar

8. In battle or business, whatever the game,
   In law or in love, it is ever the same;
   In the struggle for power, or the scramble for pelf,
   Let this be your motto,—Rely on yourself!
   For, whether the prize be a ribbon or throne,
   The victor is he who can go it alone!

   The Game of Life

9. How goes the Money?—Sure,
   I wish the ways were something fewer;
   It goes for wages, taxes, debts;
   It goes for presents, goes for bets,
   For paint, pomade, and eau de rose,—
   And that's the way the Money goes.

   How the Money Goes

10. 'Tis wise to learn; 'tis God-like to create.

    The Library

HENRY DAVID THOREAU
(1817–1862)

THOREAU, one of the transcendentalists, won the friendship of Emerson. Poet, essayist, naturalist, this great individualist drew his inspiration from a solitary life in close communion with nature. A lecturer and one-time editor of the transcendentalist journal the *Dial,* he is best known for his *Walden* and his essays championing the individual against the materialistic society which threatened his liberties.

Thoreau's work, published in two volumes in his lifetime and several posthumous volumes from his journals have made him an immortal of American literature.

1. Any man more right than his neighbors constitutes a majority of one. *The Duty of Civil Disobedience*

2. Compliments and flattery oftenest excite my contempt by the pretension they imply; for who is he that assumes to flatter me? To compliment often implies an assumption of superiority in the complimenter. It is, in fact, a subtle detraction.

3. The finest qualities in our nature, like the bloom on fruits, can be preserved only by the most delicate handling.

4. It takes two to speak the truth—one to speak, and another to hear.

5. Be not simply good; be good for something.

6. I never found the companion that was so companionable as solitude.

7. Money is not required to buy one necessity of the soul.

8. Man is the artificer of his own happiness.

9. Even the best things are not equal to their fame.

10. I would rather sit on a pumpkin, and have it all to myself, than to be crowded on a velvet cushion.

11. Water is the only drink for a wise man.

12. What a man thinks of himself, that it is which determines, or rather indicates, his fate.

13. Most of the luxuries, and many of the so-called comforts, of life are not only not indispensable, but positive hindrances to the elevation of mankind.

14. For many years I was self-appointed inspector of snow-storms and rain-storms, and did my duty faithfully.

15. Beware of all enterprises that require new clothes.

16. The swiftest traveller is he that goes afoot.

17. The man who goes alone can start today; but he who travels with another must wait till that other is ready.

18. There is no odor so bad as that which arises from goodness tainted.

19. There are a thousand hacking at the branches of evil to one who is striking at the root.

20. Time is but the stream I go a-fishing in.

21. Books must be read as deliberately and reservedly as they were written.

22. The works of the great poets have never yet been read by mankind, for only great poets can read them.

23. There is never an instant's truce between virtue and vice. Goodness is the only investment that never fails.

24. Every man is the builder of a temple, called his body.

25. While men believe in the infinite, some ponds will be thought to be bottomless.

26. Through our own recovered innocence we discern the innocence of our neighbors.

27. If a man does not keep pace with his companions, perhaps it is because he hears a different drummer. Let him step to the music which he hears, however measured or far away.

28. It is life near the bone, where it is sweetest.

29. The blue-bird carries the sky on his back.

30. The perception of beauty is a moral test.

31. The youth gets together his materials to build a bridge to the moon, or, perchance, a palace or temple on the earth, and, at length, the middle-aged man concludes to build a woodshed with them.

32. Some circumstantial evidence is very strong, as when you find a trout in the milk.

33. That man is the richest whose pleasures are the cheapest.

ELIZABETH P. PRENTISS (1818–1878)

AS publication of poems and verses by women became more and more encouraged by the proliferation of magazines and an avid body of readers [for that matter, women today are the mainstay of magazine circulation], this little gem of a lullaby was placed in print.

> Sleep, baby, sleep,
> Thy father's watching the sheep,
> Thy mother's shaking the dreamland tree,
> And down drops a little dream for thee.
>
> *Sleep, Baby, Sleep*

HENRY WHEELER SHAW (JOSH BILLINGS) (1818–1885)

FOR the first forty-two years of his life Shaw, born in Lanesboro, Massachusetts, outside Boston's intellectual pale, was a "boomer." He tried his hand at many itinerant jobs including those of farmer, explorer, coal miner and auctioneer, settling down at last in Poughkeepsie, New York. By 1863 his humorous sketches in rural dialects were appearing in local newspapers; by 1870 his popularity as a writer and lecturer were assured—"Josh Billings" was a household word.

1. Common sense is instinct, and enough of it is genius.

2. Economy is a savings bank, into which men drop pennies, and get dollars in return.

3. It is easy to assume a habit; but when you try to cast it off, it will take skin and all.

4. Incredulity is the wisdom of a fool.

5. Take the humbug out of this world, and you haven't much left to do business with.

6. A slander is like a hornet; if you cannot kill it dead at the first blow, better not strike at it.

7. There are people who are always anticipating trouble, and in this way they manage to enjoy many sorrows that never really happen to them.

8. As scarce as truth is, the supply has always been in excess of the demand.

9. It is better to know nothing than to know what ain't so.

10. Better make a weak man your enemy than your friend.

11. The wheel that squeaks the loudest
        Is the one that gets the grease.   *The Kicker*

JOSIAH GILBERT HOLLAND (1819–1881)

BEST known for his proverb that "there is no royal road . . ." Holland was another of the delightful coterie of thinkers who turned with equal facility from serious editing to the writing of novels and light verse under which lay a solid foundation of thought. A medical student and former school teacher he spent eight years with the Springfield *Republican*, until he helped found and became editor of *Scribner's Monthly*, the precursor of *Century Magazine*.

1. There is no royal road to anything. One thing at a time, all things in succession. That which grows fast withers as rapidly; that which grows slowly endures.
2. The mind grows by what it feeds on.
3. No one can disgrace us but ourselves.
4. The heart is wiser than the intellect.
5. Heaven is not reached at a single bound;
       But we build the ladder by which we rise
       From the lowly earth to the vaulted skies,
   And we mount to its summit round by round.

               .   .   .   .

   Only in dreams is a ladder thrown
       From the weary earth to the sapphire walls,
       But the dreams depart, and the vision falls,
   And the sleeper wakes on his pillow of stone.

                                    Gradatim

6. More human, more divine than we—
   In truth, half human, half divine
   Is woman when good stars agree
   To temper with their beams benign
   The hour of her nativity.

                                    Katrina

7. Nay, Whittier, thou art not old;
   Thy register a lie hath told,
   For lives devote to love and truth
   Do only multiply their youth.

                              Ten Times Seven

8. God give us men! A time like this demands
       Strong minds, great hearts, true faith, and ready
           hands;
   Men whom the lust of office does not kill;
       Men whom the spoils of office cannot buy;
   Men who possess opinions and a will;
       Men who have honor; men who will not lie;

               .   .   .   .

   Men who can stand before a demagogue

And damn his treacherous flatteries without winking;
Tall men, sun-crowned, who live above the fog
In public duty and in private thinking.

The Day's Demand

9. What is the little one thinking about?
Very wonderful things, no doubt;
Unwritten history!
Unfathomed mystery!
Yet he laughs, and cries, and eats, and drinks
And chuckles and crows, and laughs and winks,
As if his head were as full of kinks
And curious riddles as any Sphinx!

Bitter Sweet

JULIA WARD HOWE (1819–1910)

HAD Mrs. Howe written only "The Battle Hymn of the Republic," a great part of which was inspired by the sight of McClellan's army marching to battle to "John Brown's Body," she would have earned a measure of immortality, but this was no chance inspiration. From youth to old age, she wrote and helped her editor husband, Dr. Samuel Gridley Howe. She was elected the first woman member of the American Academy of Arts and Letters.

1. I gave my son a palace
    and a kingdom to control:
The palace of his body,
    The kingdom of his soul.

Palace and Kingdom

2. Mine eyes have seen the glory of the coming of the Lord;
He is trampling out the vintage where the grapes of wrath
    are stored;
He hath loosed the fateful lightning of His terrible, swift
    sword;
His truth is marching on.

.   .   .   .   .

In the beauty of the lilies Christ was born, across the sea,
With a glory in His bosom that transfigures you and me;
As He died to make men holy, let us die to make men free.
    While God is marching on.
                                    Battle Hymn of the Republic
3. Don't trouble more to celebrate this natal day of mine,
    But keep the grasp of fellowship which warms us more
        than wine.
    Let us thank the lavish hand that gives world beauty to
        our eyes,
    And bless the days that saw us young, and years that made
        us wise.
                                    Growing Old

JAMES RUSSELL LOWELL (1819–1891)

AFTER being chosen class poet of Harvard, 1838, Lowell ploughed through three more years to a law degree, only to abandon that profession and turn to the writing and editing, teaching and diplomacy, which made him a towering figure in nineteenth-century American life. Highly successful at the age of thirty-five, he went abroad for a year to study, and on his return succeeded Longfellow as Smith professor of French and Spanish at Harvard, a post he held actively for ten years, the title of which he held ten more. He was hardly settled there when he also became the first editor of the *Atlantic Monthly*. He only seemed to "retire" from letters in 1877, when he was appointed Minister to Spain. In three years he went as Minister to London, where he remained for another five. In those posts he was credited with creating a new respect for Americans.

1. There is no good in arguing with the inevitable. The only argument available with an east wind is to put on your overcoat.

2. Compromise makes a good umbrella, but a poor roof; it is a temporary expedient, often wise in party politics, almost sure to be unwise in statesmanship.

3. One thorn of experience is worth a whole wilderness of warning.

4. The only faith that wears well and holds its color in all weathers is that which is woven of conviction and set with the sharp mordant of experience.

5. It is curious how tyrannical the habit of reading is.

6. Incredulity robs us of many pleasures, and gives us nothing in return.

7. In the scale of the destinies, brawn will never weigh so much as brain.

8. The devil loves nothing better than the intolerance of reformers, and dreads nothing so much as their charity and patience.

9. The foolish and the dead alone never change their opinions.

10. Blessed are they who have nothing to say, and who cannot be persuaded to say it.

11. Sincerity is impossible, unless it pervades the whole being, and the pretence of it saps the very foundation of character.

12. Not suffering but faint heart is worst of woes.

13. The story of any one man's real experience finds its startling parallel in that of every one of us.

14. Solitude is as needful to the imagination as society is wholesome for the character.

15. From the days of the first grandfather, everybody has remembered a golden age behind him!

16. Notoriety may be achieved in a narrow sphere, but fame demands for its evidence a more distant and prolonged reverberation.

17. A wise skepticism is the first attribute of a good critic.

18. There is no better ballast for keeping the mind steady on its keel, and saving it from all risk of crankiness, than business.

19. Puritanism, believing itself quick with the seed of religious liberty, laid, without knowing it, the egg of democracy.

20. It was in making education not only common to all, but in some sense compulsory on all, that the destiny of the free republics of America was practically settled.

21. Every man feels instinctively that all the beautiful sentiments in the world weigh less than a single lovely action.

22. Things always seem fairer when we look back at them, and it is out of that inaccessible tower of the past that Longing leans and beckons.

23. It is by presence of mind in untried emergencies that the native metal of a man is tested.

24. Mishaps are like knives, that either serve us or cut us, as we grasp them by the blade or the handle.

25. No man, I suspect, ever lived long in the country without being bitten by these meteorological ambitions. He likes to be hotter or colder, to have been more deeply snowed up, to have more trees and larger blown down than his neighbors.

26. Let us be of good cheer, however, remembering that the misfortunes hardest to bear are those which never come.

27. There are few brains that would not be better for living on their own fat for a little while.

28. Democracy gives every man a right to be his own oppressor.

29. Earth has its price for what earth gives us,
  The beggar is taxed for a corner to die in,
The priest hath his fee who comes and shrives us,
  We bargain for the graves we lie in;
At the devil's booth are all things sold,
  Each ounce of dross costs its ounce of gold;
For a cap and bells our lives we pay,
  Bubbles we buy with a whole soul's tasking,
'Tis heaven alone that is given away,
  'Tis only God may be had for the asking.
No price is set on the lavish summer;
  June may be had by the poorest comer.

.   .   .   .

And what is so rare as a day in June?
  Then, if ever, come perfect days;
Then Heaven tries the earth if it be in tune,
  And over it softly her warm ear lays.
                                The Vision of Sir Launfal

30. Nature, they say, doth dote,

And cannot make a man
Save in some out-worn plan,
Repeating us by rote.

Ode at Harvard Commemoration

31. Great truths are portions of the soul of man;
Great souls are portions of Eternity.

Sonnet VI

32. Be noble! and the nobleness that lies
In other men, sleeping, but never dead,
Will rise in majesty to meet thine own.

Sonnet IV

33. No man is born into the world whose work
Is not born with him; there is always work,
And tools to work withal, for those who will:
And blessed are the horny hands of toil!

A Glance Behind the Curtain

34. Once to every man and nation comes the moment to decide,
In the strife of Truth with Falsehood, for the good or evil side.

. . . .

Truth forever on the scaffold, Wrong forever on the throne.

. . . .

Then to side with Truth is noble when we share her wretched crust,
Ere her cause bring fame and profit, and 'tis prosperous to be just;
Then it is the brave man chooses, while the coward stands aside,
Doubting in his abject spirit, till his Lord is crucified.

. . . .

New occasions teach new duties: time makes ancient good uncouth;
They must upward still, and onward, who would keep abreast of truth.

The Present Crisis

35. I've thought very often 'twould be a good thing,
   In all public collections of books, if a wing
   Were set off by itself, like the seas from the dry lands,
   Marked *Literature suited to desolate islands.*

    . . . .

   There comes Emerson first, whose rich words, every one,
   Are like gold nails in temples to hang trophies on;
   Whose prose is grand verse, while his verse, the Lord
      knows,
   Is some of it pr— No, 'tis not even prose.

    . . . .

   And I honor the man who is willing to sink
   Half his present repute for the freedom to think,
   And, when he has thought, be his cause strong or weak,
   Will risk t' other half for the freedom to speak.

    . . . .

   There comes Poe, with his raven, like Barnaby Rudge,
   Three fifths of him genius and two fifths sheer fudge.

    . . . .

   Nature fits all her children with something to do,
   He who would write and can't write, can surely review.
               A Fable for Critics

36. The wise man could ask no more of Fate
   Than to be simple, modest, manly, true,
   Safe from the Many, honored by the Few;
   To count as naught in World, or Church, or State;
   But inwardly in secret to be great.
             Sonnet: Jeffries Wyman

HERMAN MELVILLE (1819–1891)

IF this collection were being made within ten or twenty years after Melville's death, he probably would not be included. *Typee* and *Omoo*, his first novels, were criticized but read. The obscurantism of later works—particularly *Pierre* and *Moby Dick*—put them above his readers' understanding until there was a revival of interest in the 1920's. Melville had the soundest of backgrounds for realistic writing, having served on a whaler, lived among South Sea savages. In fact, he experienced so many adventures that books now current on his life are almost as interesting as his writings. Even so his popularity today rests far more on contemporary interest in the study of psychology and symbol in the novel than on his gift for graphic and powerful description of life in remote parts of the world.

1. There is no faith, and no stoicism, and no philosophy, that a mortal man can possibly evoke, which will stand the final test in a real impassioned onset of Life and Passion upon him. Faith and philosophy are air, but events are brass. *Pierre*

2. Thou belongest to that hopeless, sallow tribe which no wine of this world will ever warm; and for whom even Pale Sherry would be too rosy-strong; but with whom one sometimes loves to sit, and feel poor-devilish, too; and grow convivial upon tears; and say to them bluntly, with full eyes and empty glasses, and in not altogether unpleasant sadness— Give it up, Sub-Subs! For by how much the more pains ye take to please the world, by so much the more shall ye for ever go thankless.

. . . .

The Nantucketer, out of sight of land, furls his sail and lays him to his rest, while under his very pillow rush herds of walruses and whales.

. . . .

A whale ship was my Yale College and my Harvard.

. . . .

Thou great democratic God! who didst not refuse to the swart convict, Bunyan, the pale poetic pearl; Thou who didst clothe with doubly hammered leaves of finest gold, the stumped and paupered arm of old Cervantes; Thou who didst pick up Andrew Jackson from the pebbles; who didst hurl him upon a war-horse; who didst thunder him higher than a throne!

. . . .

The starred and stately nights seem haughty dames in jewelled velvets, nursing at home in lonely pride the memory of their absent conquering Earls, the golden helmeted suns!

. . . .

. . . the choice hidden handful of the Divine Inert

. . . .

Where lies the final harbor, whence we unmoor no more?
Moby Dick: Preface, the Sub-Sub Librarian

WILLIAM ROSS WALLACE (1819–1881)

THIS lawyer-poet, author of poetical romances and stirring patriotic songs, contributed to most of the leading periodicals of his day; but we remember him for just two lines in a poem—lines now a proverb.

The hand that rocks the cradle
Is the hand that rules the world.
The Hand That Rules the World

WALT WHITMAN (1819–1892)

THE first twelve-poem edition of Leaves of Grass first published by Whitman himself was ignored; it was not until the second edition appeared that it drew such attention and criticism for its daring subject matter and metric freedom. At various times an editor, hospital nurse and government worker, Whitman's experience in the world of men as well as literature (he read widely in the philosophy of America, Europe and the Far East) brought to all his work great human understanding. He was a pantheist, a mystic and a frank admirer of the human body; his greatest accomplishment was to give a new and broader reach to all American poetry.

1. The United States themselves are essentially the greatest poem. . . . Here at last is something in the doings of man that corresponds with the broadcast doings of the day and night . . .

The proof of a poet is that his country absorbs him as affectionately as he has absorbed it.

Preface to *Leaves of Grass,* 1855

2. Language is not an abstract construction of the learned, or of dictionary-makers, but is something arising out of the work, needs, ties, joys, affections, tastes, of long generations of humanity, and has its bases broad and low, close to the ground.

Slang in America

3. Did you too, O friend, suppose democracy was only for elections, for politics, and for a party name?

4. None of the artists or pictures has caught the deep, though subtle and indirect expression of this man's face. There is something else there. One of the great portrait painters of two or three centuries ago is needed.

. . . .

I never see that man without feeling that he is one to become personally attach'd to, for his combination of purest, heartiest tenderness, and native western form of manliness. . . .

. . . .

He leaves for America's history and biography, so far, not only its most dramatic reminiscence—he leaves, in my opinion, the greatest, best, most characteristic, artistic, moral personality.

Notes on Abraham Lincoln

5. Political democracy, as it exists and practically works in America, with all its threatening evils, supplies a training-school for making first-class men. It is life's gymnasium, not of good only, but of all.

Democratic Vistas

6. To have great poets, there must be great audiences, too.

7. No really great song can ever attain full purport till long after the death of its singer—till it has accrued and incorporated the many passions, many joys and sorrows, it has itself aroused.

8. Once fully enslaved, no nation, state, city of this earth, ever afterward resumes its liberty. *November Bows*

9. I will write the evangel-poem of comrades and of love.

. . . .

I say the whole earth and all the stars in the sky are for religion's sake.

. . . .

None has begun to think how divine he himself is, and
    how certain the future is.

.   .   .   .

I say the real and permanent grandeur of these States must
    be their religion.

.   .   .   .

Nothing can happen more beautiful than death.

.   .   .   .

Whoever you are, to you endless announcements!
                      Starting from Paumanok

10. I celebrate myself and sing myself,
    And what I assume you shall assume.

.   .   .   .

I loaf and invite my soul.

.   .   .   .

And every atom belonging to me as good as belongs to
    you.

.   .   .   .

I have no mockings or arguments; I witness and wait.

.   .   .   .

I am an acme of things accomplished, and I am an enclo-
    sure of things to be.

.   .   .   .

Behold, I do not give lectures or a little charity,
    When I give I give myself.

.   .   .   .

All goes onward and outward, nothing collapses,
And to die is different from what anyone supposed, and
    luckier.

.   .   .   .

Whether I come to my own today or in ten thousand or
    ten million years,
I can cheerfully take it now, or with equal cheerfulness
    I can wait.

I believe a leaf of grass is no less than the journeywork
    of the stars.

.   .   .

And the tree-toad is a chef-d'oeuvre for the highest, . . .
And a mouse is miracle enough to stagger sextillions of
    infidels.

.   .   .

I think I could turn and live with animals, they are so
    placid and self-contain'd.

.   .   .

The clock indicates the moment—but what does eternity
    indicate?

.   .   .

In the faces of men and women I see God.

.   .   .

I sound my barbaric yawp over the roofs of the world.
        Song of Myself

11. If anything is sacred the human body is sacred.
        Children of Adam

12. A great city is that which has the greatest men and women.
        Song of the Broad-Axe

13. All architecture is what you do to it when you look upon
    it.

.   .   .

All music is what awakes from you when you are re-
    minded by the instruments.
        A Song for Occupations

14. In this broad earth of ours,
Amid the measureless grossness and the slag,
Enclosed and safe within its central heart,
Nestles the seed of perfection.
        Song of the Universal

15. Roaming in thought over the Universe, I saw the little
    that if Good steadily hastening toward immortality,

And the vast that is Evil I saw hastening to merge itself
and become lost and dead.

Roaming in Thought after Reading Hegel

16. Give me the splendid silent sun with all his beams full-
dazzling!

Give Me the Splendid Silent Sun

17. When lilacs last in the dooryard bloom'd,
And the great star early droop'd in the western sky in the
night,
I mourn'd—and yet shall mourn with ever-returning
spring.

When Lilacs Last in the Dooryard Bloomed

18. O Captain! my Captain! our fearful trip is done,
The ship has weather'd every rock, the prize we sought
is won,
The Port is near, the bells I hear, the people all exulting,

.   .   .   .

The ship is anchor'd safe and sound, its voyage closed
and done,
From fearful trip the victor ship comes in with object
won; . . . .

O Captain! My Captain!

19. No more for him life's stormy conflict,
Nor victory, nor defeat—no more time's dark events,
Charging like ceaseless clouds across the sky.

Hush'd be the Camps To-day

20. The whole theory of the universe is directed unerringly
to one single individual—namely to You.

By Blue Ontario's Shore

21. Joyous we too launch out on trackless seas,
Fearless for unknown shores.

Passage to India

22. What do you suppose will satisfy the soul, except to walk
free and own no superior?

Laws for Creations

23. To me every hour of the light and dark is a miracle,
    Every cubic inch of space is a miracle.

Miracles

24. Society waits unform'd, and is for a while between things
    ended and things begun.

Thoughts

25. I swear I think there is nothing but immortality.

To Think of Time

26. This is the hour O soul, thy free flight into the wordless,
    Away from books, away from art, the day erased, the
    lesson done,
    Thee fully forth emerging, silent, gazing, pondering the
    themes thou lovest best,
    Night, sleep, death and the stars.

A Clear Midnight

27. Our life is closed, our life begins,
    The long, long anchorage we leave,
    The ship is clear at last, she leaps!
    She swiftly courses from the shore,
    Joy, shipmate, joy.

Joy, Shipmate, Joy!

28. I announce the great individual, fluid as Nature, chaste,
    affectionate, compassionate, fully armed;
    I announce a life that shall be copious, vehement, spiritual,
    bold,
    And I announce an end that shall lightly and joyfully
    meet its translation.

So Long!

29. I am the Poem of Earth, said the voice of the rain,
    Eternal I rise impalpable out of the land and the bottom-
    less sea.

The Voice of the Rain

BROADENING HORIZONS

SUSAN BROWNELL ANTHONY (1820–1906)

THIS section opens with the words of the colorful and embattled crusader for woman suffrage who outraged politicians and some of her own sex, became the darling of the cartoonists, and yet won serious attention for her cause.

1. Modern invention has banished the spinning-wheel, and the same law of progress makes the woman of today a different woman from her grandmother.

2. The only question left to be settled now is: Are women persons?

ALICE CARY (1820–1871)

MISS Cary and her sister, Phoebe, four years her junior, first published a volume of poems in 1849, under their joint names, while they lived in the "western" city of Cincinnati. With recognition, particularly by Horace Greeley, they moved to New York. We often quote from Alice Cary without realizing the source.

1. There must be rough, cold weather,
    And winds and rains so wild;
Not all good things together
    Come to us here, my child.

.   .   .   .

So when some dear joy loses
    Its beauteous summer glow,
Think how the roots of roses
    Are kept alive in the snow.

November

2. My soul is full of whispered song,
    My blindness is my sight;

The shadows that I feared so long
  Are all alive with light.

Dying Hymn

3. Three little bugs in a basket,
  And hardly room for two.

Three Little Bugs

THEODORE O'HARA (1820–1867)

O'HARA'S poetry scarcely sur-
vived him, with one great and
notable exception, inspired by the
sacrifices made by both sides in the
Battle of Buena Vista, 1847, during
the War with Mexico.

The muffled drum's sad roll has beat
  The soldier's last tattoo;
No more on life's parade shall meet
  The brave and fallen few.
On Fame's eternal camping ground,
  Their silent tents are spread,
And Glory guards, with solemn round,
  The bivouac of the dead.

.   .   .   .

Sons of the Dark and Bloody ground,
  Ye must not slumber there,
Where stranger steps and tongues resound
  Along the heedless air.

The Bivouac of the Dead

GEORGE FREDERICK ROOT (1820–1895)

ROOT, as an educator, contributed
greatly to the development of
American choral music. Also a
composer of over 200 sentimental
ballads, he rose above himself to
create like O'Hara, one of the most
stirring ballads that came out of the
Civil War.

Yes, we'll rally round the flag, boys, we'll rally once again,
  Shouting the battle-cry of Freedom.
We will rally from the hill-side, we'll gather from the plain,
  Shouting the battle-cry of Freedom.

Battle Cry of Freedom

WILLIAM TECUMSEH SHERMAN
(1820–1891)

THIS brilliant military commander, who might have been President of the United States had he chosen, is most remembered as the commanding general of the "March to the Sea" through Georgia—a military campaign ordered to cut the South's communications in the Civil War, and otherwise convince the civilian population of the futility of continuing resistance. The devastation was great, but later years have brought exaggerated tales of atrocities. It is a matter of record that Sherman combined military genius with a downright hatred of war.

1. War is cruel and you cannot refine it.

2. War at best is barbarism.

3. I am tired and sick of war. Its glory is all moonshine. It is only those who have neither fired a shot nor heard the shrieks and groans of the wounded who cry aloud for blood, more vengeance, more desolation. War is hell.

4. If nominated [for the Presidency] I will not accept; if elected I will not serve.

MARY BAKER EDDY
(1821–1910)

HAD Mrs. Eddy, the discoverer and founder of Christian Science, written only as a well-educated and deeply sympathetic author and poet, she would have clearly won recognition as a literary figure in her age. The founding of a church necessarily provoked controversy and criticism. One recalls that on her passing Clara Barton, who almost single-handed founded the American National Red Cross, called her "the greatest woman of her age."

In 1963 the annual report of The Mother Church, The First Church of Christ Scientist, Boston,

Massachusetts, noted that branches of the Mother Church (not counting Societies) stood at an all-time high of 3,282. In addition, the *Christian Science Monitor,* an international daily newspaper founded by Mrs. Eddy, ranked professionally among the world's leading papers.

1. To those leaning on the sustaining infinite, today is big with blessings.

. . . .

2. The prayer that reforms the sinner and heals the sick is an absolute faith that all things are possible to God,—a spiritual understanding of Him, an unselfed love.

. . . .

3. Christian Science explains all cause and effect as mental, not physical.

. . . .

4. The basis of all health, sinlessness, and immortality is the great fact that God is the only Mind; and this Mind must be not merely believed, it must be understood.

. . . .

5. Being is holiness, harmony, immortality. It is already proved that a knowledge of this, even in small degree, will uplift the physical and moral standard of mortals, will increase longevity, will purify and elevate character. Thus progress will finally destroy all error, and bring immortality to light.

. . . .

6. Divine Love always has met and always will meet every human need.

. . . .

7. God is incorporeal, divine, supreme, infinite Mind, Spirit, Soul, Principle, Life, Truth, Love.   *Science and Health*

8. Science defines man as immortal, as coexistent and coeternal with God, as made in His own image and likeness.

Retrospection and Introspection

9. To live so as to keep human consciousness in constant relation with the divine, the spiritual, and the eternal, is to individualize infinite power; and this is Christian Science.

The First Church of Christ, Scientist, and Miscellany

10. It matters not what be thy lot,
     So Love doth guide;
   For storm or shine, pure peace is thine,
     Whate'er betide.

Satisfied

.11. Blest Christmas morn, though murky clouds
       Pursue thy way,
    Thy light was born where storm enshrouds
       Nor dawn nor day.

Christmas Morn

12. Shepherd, show me how to go
       O'er the hillside steep,
   How to gather, how to sow,
       How to feed Thy sheep;
   I will listen for Thy voice,
       Lest my footsteps stray,
   I will follow and rejoice
       All the rugged way.

Shepherd, Show Me How to Go

13. O'er waiting harp-strings of the mind,
       There sweeps a strain,
   Low, sad, and sweet, whose measures bind
       The pow'r of pain.

.   .   .   .

   My prayer, some daily good to do,
       To Thine, for Thee—
   An off'ring pure of Love, whereto
       God leadeth me.

O'er Waiting Harp-Strings of the Mind

WILLIAM HENRY VANDERBILT
(1821–1885)

THIS son of the founder of the family fortune and president of the New York Central Railroad, was quoted as making one exclamation which [accurate or not] some think epitomized the spirit of conquest of

America's first money-makers. In fairness to this Vanderbilt it must be told that he distributed $100,000 among his workers in appreciation for their loyalty to him during the railroad strike of 1877 and contributed much of his wealth to charitable projects.

The public be damned!

ULYSSES SIMPSON GRANT (1822–1885)

THE victorious Civil War general and eighteenth President was a man of many contradictions and probably would have a greater reputation had he not been elected to the country's highest office in 1868. His term was characterized by corruption and scandal and he gave political appointments to friends without regard to ability. He had to cope with times which he seemed not to understand—particularly the machinations of unprincipled businessmen using every means to make fortunes in the economic wake of the Civil War and the graft of his own subordinates. One recalls sentimentally that one friend, Samuel Clemens, helped the president to complete his autobiography while he was dying of cancer in order to pay his debts.

1. No terms except an unconditional and immediate surrender can be accepted. *At Fort Donelson, 1862*

2. I propose to fight it out on this line, if it takes all summer. *To President Lincoln, May 11, 1864*

3. Let us have peace. *Accepting Presidential Nomination, May 29, 1868*

4. I know no method to secure the repeal of bad or obnoxious laws so effective as their stringent execution. *Inaugural Address, 1869*

5. Leave the matter of religion to the family altar, the church, and the private school, supported entirely by private contributions. Keep the Church and the State forever separate. *Speech, 1875*

6. Labor disgraces no man; unfortunately you occasionally find men disgrace labor. *Speech, 1877*

EDWARD EVERETT HALE
(1822–1909)

THIS Unitarian clergyman and prolific writer, famous as author of "The Man Without a Country," published that work anonymously in 1863 in the Atlantic Monthly as an inspirational patriotic piece. Born in Boston and educated at Harvard, he was a nephew of Edward Everett, the famous Massachusetts orator.

1. Behind all these men you have to do with, behind officers, and government, and people even, there is the Country Herself, your Country . . . you belong to Her as you belong to your own mother. Stand by Her, boy, as you would stand by your mother.

.   .   .   .

He loved his country as no other man has loved her, but no man deserved less at her hands.   *The Man Without a Country*

2. It is not necessary to finish your sentences in a crowd, but by a sort of mumble, omitting sibilants and dentals. This, indeed, if your words fail you, answers even in public extempore speech, but better where other talking is going on.

3. To look up and not down,
   To look forward and not back,
   To look out and not in, and
   To lend a hand.

Ten Times One Is Ten

RUTHERFORD B. HAYES
(1822–1893)

IN his administration of his office the nineteenth President tried hard to offset a contest in which historians still believe that Republican political machines in the States "rigged" his election by counting ballots in order to keep victory from the Democratic candidate, Samuel J. Tilden. But his personal character was good and he left one often-quoted remark dealing with political morals.

He serves his party best who serves the country best.

Inaugural Address, 1877

BERNARD ELLIOTT BEE (1824–1861)

NAME Thomas Jonathan Jackson to a friend and, unless he is unusually well informed about the Civil War, he will ask who that is. But to say "Stonewall Jackson" is another matter indeed: almost everyone knows this designation of the greastest of Lee's commanders, who, on the night of May 2, 1863, was mortally wounded by his own men. He came by his popular name at the first Battle of Bull Run, July 21, 1861 through a remark of General Bee just before Bee was mortally wounded in this very battle.

There is Jackson, standing like a stone wall.

JULIA FLETCHER CARNEY (1823–1908)

THIS poet and writer is identified with one of the most famous and original of American sayings, woven into a catchy little poem written when she was twenty-two years old.

Little drops of water,
    Little grains of sand,
Make the mighty ocean
    And the pleasant land.

So the little moments,
    Humble though they be,

Make the mighty ages
   Of eternity!

.   .   .   .

Little deeds of kindness,
   Little words of love,
Help to make earth happy,
   Like the heaven above.

Little Things

WILLIAM M. TWEED (1823–1878)

THIS leader of Tammany Hall, whose Ring stole millions of dollars and so controlled New York politics that he seemed untouchable for many years, at last was convicted and sent to prison, where he died. The "Boss" was credited in 1871 with making this statement:

As long as I count the votes what are you going to do about it? Say.

GEORGE WILLIAM CURTIS (1824–1892)

THIS gentle, philosophical editor, orator and reformer conducted for forty years a column of comment in *Harper's New Monthly Magazine* and, in addition, after 1863, was political editor of *Harper's Weekly*. Noted first for his participation in the crusade against slavery, he later championed political reform and woman suffrage.

1. While we read history we make history.

.   .   .   .

Every great crisis of human history is a pass of Thermopylae, and there is always a Leonidas and his three hundred to die in it, if they can not conquer.

The Call of Freedom

2. Imagination is as good as many voyages—and how much cheaper.

3. Every mother who has lost an infant has gained a child of immortal youth.

4. I think that to have known one good old man—one man who, through the chances and rubs of a long life, has carried his heart in his hand, like a palm branch, waving all discords into peace, helps our faith in God, in ourselves, and in each other, more than many sermons.

5. Happiness is speechless.

6. It is not observed in history that families improve with time. It is rather discovered that the whole matter is like a comet, of which the brightest part is the head; and the tail, although long and luminous, is gradually shaded into obscurity.

7. The pride of ancestry increases in the ratio of distance.

8. Love is the coldest of critics. *2–8: Prue and I*

CHARLES GODFREY LELAND
(HANS BREITMANN) (1824–1903)

THIS man of many facets, most remembered for his poetry, wrote more than fifty books based on travels and his study of folklore, and is credited with having introduced industrial and craft arts into American schools. Leland varied the usual academic pattern of celebrated writers of his day by attending not Harvard, but Princeton (still known in his days as the College of New Jersey).

1. To Paradise, the Arabs say,
      Satan could never find the way
         Until the peacock led him in.

The Peacock

2. And softly came the fair young queen
         O'er mountain, dale, and dell;
      And where her golden light was seen
         An emerald shadow fell.
   The good-wife opened the window wide,
   The good man spanned his plough;

'Tis time to run, 'tis time to ride
For Spring is with us now.

Spring

3. If all the world the world must see
       As all the world hath seen,
   Then it were better for the world
       That the world had never been.

The World and the World

4. The greatest sharp some day will find a sharper wit;
   It always makes the devil laugh to see a biter bit;
   It takes two Spaniards any day to come a Yankee o'er—
   Even two like Don Alonzo Estaban San Salvador.

El Capitan-General

5. They saw a Dream of Loveliness descending from the
   train.

．　　．　　．　　．

   The brave deserve the lovely—every woman may be won.

The Masher

WILLIAM ALLEN BUTLER
(1825–1902)

NEVER as famous as many of his colleagues, Butler nevertheless was a popular writer of verse, with wide range of descriptive feeling:

1. We read Virginia's blazoned roll
       Of heroes, and forthwith
   Greets us upon the starry scroll
       That homeliest name,—John Smith!

Virginia's Virgin

2. No record of her high descent
       There needs, nor memory of her name;
   Enough that Raphael's colors blent
       To give her features deathless fame.

Incognita of Raphael

3. Dresses for breakfasts, and dinners, and balls;
   Dresses to sit in, and stand in, and walk in;
   Dresses to dance in, and flirt in, and talk in;
   Dresses in which to do nothing at all;
   Dresses for Winter, Spring, Summer, and Fall.

This same Miss McFlimsey, of Madison Square,
The last time we met was in utter despair,
Because she had nothing whatever to wear!

Nothing to Wear

BAYARD TAYLOR (1825–1878)

TAYLOR'S verse, of which the best remembered is "Bedouin Love Song," though not great poetry, earned him a career such as few poets achieve—a steady job with the New York *Tribune* on assignment to travel and write. He traveled throughout most of the world, pioneering as an explorer of the interior of Egypt. Oddly enough it has long been forgotten, except in reference works, that a translation of Goethe's *Faust* won him such distinction that in 1878, just before his death in Berlin, he was appointed Minister to Germany.

1. I love thee, I love but thee,
   With a love that shall not die
      Till the sun grows cold,
      And the stars are old,
   And the leaves of the Judgment Book unfold!

Bedouin Song

2. They sang of love, and not of fame;
      Forgot was Britain's glory;
   Each heart recalled a different name,
      But all sang "Annie Laurie."

The Song of the Camp

3. The violet loves a sunny bank,
      The cowslip loves the lea;

The scarlet creeper loves the elm,
But I love—thee.

Proposal

4. For every sentence uttered, a million more are dumb;
   Men's lives are chains of chances, and History their sun.

Napoleon at Gotha

5. But who will watch my lilies,
   When their blossoms open white?
   By day the sun shall be sentry,
   And the moon and the stars by night.

The Garden of Roses

6. Round and round the glorious sun
   Walks with level steps the spray,
   Through his vestibule of the Day.

April in the Cloven Pine

STEPHEN COLLINS FOSTER
(1826–1864)

SON of a poor family and born in part of what is now Pittsburgh, Pennsylvania, Foster lacked musical education but had a native talent for both lyrics and composition that won the attention of E. P. Christy, manager of a famous minstrel troupe. In fact, Christy signed the first published version of "Old Folks at Home." Never well rewarded for his work, and a heavy drinker, Foster died in a public hospital in New York as a result of injuries suffered in a fall.

1. Old dog Tray's ever faithful;
   Grief can not drive him away;
   He is gentle. He is kind—
   I'll never, never find
   A better friend than old dog Tray.

Old Dog Tray

2. Oh! darkies, how my heart grows weary,
   Far from the old folks at home.

The Old Folks at Home

166 / *Stephen Collins Foster*

3. The day goes by like a shadow o'er the heart,
   With sorrow where all was delight;
The time has come when the darkies have to part:
   Then my old Kentucky Home, good night!

My Old Kentucky Home

4. Where are the hearts once so happy and free?
   The children so dear that I held upon my knee?
Gone to the shore where my soul has longed to go,
I hear their gentle voices calling, "Old Black Joe!"

Old Black Joe

5. O, Susanna! O, don't you cry for me,
   I've come from Alabama, wid my banjo on my knee.

O, Susanna

6. I dream of Jeanie with the light brown hair,
      Borne like a vapor on the summer air;
   I see her tripping where the bright streams play,
      Happy as the daisies that dance on her way.

Jeanie with the Light Brown Hair

7. Beautiful dreamer, wake unto me,
   Starlight and dewdrop are waiting for thee;
Sounds of the rude world heard in the day,
Lulled by the moonlight have all passed away.

Beautiful Dreamer

8. Come Where My Love Lies Dreaming

Title and Refrain

EDWARD STUYVESANT BRAGG
(1827–1912)

IT is a commonplace remark that a good man may be judged by the enemies he has made. The expression came from an inspired line of oratory by Bragg, a delegate to the Democratic National Convention, at Chicago, July 9, 1884, who seconded the nomination of Grover A. Cleveland—later elected President of the United States.

They love him most for the enemies he has made.

FRANCIS MILES FINCH (1827–1907)

THE multi-talented nineteenth-century American is found again in Finch, who is remembered by some as a distinguished judge in New York and later Dean of the Cornell Law School; by others, as a poet, distinguished for publications in the *Atlantic Monthly,* and author of one well-remembered evocation of the Civil War, written in 1867.

These in the robings of glory,
　　Those in the gloom of defeat,
All with the battle-blood gory,
　　In the dusk of eternity meet:
　　　　Under the sod and the dew,
　　　　Waiting the judgment-day;
　　　　Under the laurel, the Blue,
　　　　Under the willow, the Gray.

The Blue and the Gray

CHARLES ELIOT NORTON (1827–1908)

DR. Norton was part of the Harvard-Cambridge tradition by birth, by education and, after a time as co-editor with James Russell Lowell of the *North American Review,* still later as Harvard professor of the history of art. A life-long scholar, noted for a prose translation of Dante, and many books of criticism dealing with other savants. His own comments were confined principally to letters and papers and later gathered into book form by his daughter.

1. It is perhaps the highest distinction of the Greeks that they recognized the indissoluble connection of beauty and goodness.

2. The artistic temperament is not a national trait of the English race. Our complex and exciting civilization has, indeed,

168 / *Charles Eliot Norton*

developed, especially in America, a sensitiveness of nervous organization which often wears the semblance of the artistic temperament, and shows itself in manual dexterity and refined technical skill. And thus tends to make mere workmanship, mere excellence of execution, the common test of merit in a work of fine arts.

3. The refuge from pessimism is the good men and women existing at any time in the world,—they keep faith and happiness alive.

4. Whatever your occupation may be and however crowded your hours with affairs, do not fail to secure at least a few minutes every day for refreshment of your inner life with a bit of poetry.

ROSCOE CONKLING (1829–1888)

THIS New York political leader and senator attempted to nominate President Grant for a third term, at the Republican National Convention held in 1880. Some would dispute his description of this former President, but in his nominating speech he coined an expression.

He will hew to the line of right, let the chips fall where they may.

JOSEPH JEFFERSON (1829–1905)

IN 1870 an elderly actor named George Holland died and his friends, arranging funeral services, were rebuffed by an unnamed church that refused to hold services for an actor. Joseph Jefferson, himself a famous star, then arranged for the funeral to be held at the Church of the Transfiguration, New York City, and by his exclamation of gratitude gave it a name—The Little Church Around the Corner.

God bless the little church around the corner.

CARL SCHURZ (1829–1906)

SCHURZ had to flee his native Germany at the age of twenty; he was wanted for participation in revolutionary activities while still a student at the University of Bonn. In 1852 he emigrated to the United States and thus America gained a distinguished editor, author, senator from Missouri, devoted supporter of Lincoln, and at his political peak a member of the Cabinet. Schurz's whole life was devoted, as it were, to expressing the ideals of America.

1. Cordial international understanding rests upon a very simple, natural and solid basis. We rejoice with the nations of the Old World in all their successes, all their prosperity, and all their happiness, and we profoundly and earnestly sympathize with them whenever a misfortune overtakes them. But one thing we shall never think of doing, and that is, interfering in their affairs.

. . . . .

The Old World and the New will ever live in harmonious accord as long as we do not try to jump over their fences and they do not try to jump over ours. . . . The only danger ahead of us might be that arising from altogether too sentimental a fondness for one another which may lead us into lovers' quarrels and jealousies.   *Speech, New York, 1881*

2. Ideals are like stars; you will not succeed in touching them with your hands. But like the seafaring man on the desert of waters, you choose them as your guides, and following them you will reach your destiny.   *Address, 1859*

3. Our country, right or wrong. When right, to be kept right; when wrong, to be put right.   *Address, 1899*

EMILY DICKINSON (1830–1886)

IN any handful of names compiled to represent "great" American poets —and this is truer perhaps at this writing than in the past—Miss Dickinson must be present, both as a representative and as a pattern-maker. This enigmatic daughter of an Amherst professor, who lived most of her adult life in virtual seclusion in her father's house, left such a mass of writings and notes, unpublished at her death, that studies still continue. It may be expected that publishers in the future will bring out yet "new" Dickinson poems.

1. And so upon this wise I prayed,—
    Great Spirit, give to me
A heaven not so large as yours
    But large enough for me.

A Prayer

2. Faith in a fine invention
    For gentlemen who see;
But Microscopes are prudent
    In an emergency.

.   .   .   .

Much madness is divinest sense
    To a discerning eye;
Much sense the starkest madness.

Poems

3. Success is counted sweetest
By those who ne'er succeed.

Success

4. If I can stop one heart from breaking,
    I shall not live in vain;
If I can ease one life the aching,
    Or cool one pain,
Or help one fainting robin
    Unto his nest again,
I shall not live in vain.

If I Can Stop One Heart from Breaking

5. I taste a liquor never brewed,
    From tankards scooped in pearl;

In a Library

6. He ate and drank the precious words,
    His spirit grew robust;
He knew no more that he was poor,

Nor that his frame was dust.
He danced along the dingy days,
And this bequest of wings
Was but a book. What liberty
A loosened spirit brings.

A Book

7. The pedigree of honey
   Does not concern the bee;
   A clover, any time, to him
   Is aristocracy.

Nature

8. Afraid? Of whom am I afraid?
   Not death; for who is he?
   The porter of my father's lodge
   As much abasheth me.

Time and Eternity

9. How dreary to be somebody!
   How public, like a frog
   To tell your name the livelong day
   To an admiring bog!

Life

10. We never know how high we are
    Till we are called to rise;
    And then, if we are true to plan,
    Our statures touch the skies.

Aspiration

GEORGE GRAHAM VEST
(1830–1904)

WHEN Vest retired in 1903 after twenty-four years of service as a senator from Missouri, it could truly be said that never in that long career did he say or do a thing that might be considered distinguished. Yet he already was "immortalized" as the result of a brief plea made to a jury, when he was a young lawyer, in a suit over a killed dog.

In fact, he devoted most of his public appearances to repeating the plea for audiences that never seemed to grow tired of it.

Gentlemen of the Jury: The best friend a man has in the world may turn against him and become his enemy. His son or daughter that he has reared with loving care may prove ungrateful. Those who are nearest and dearest to us, those whom we trust with our happiness and our good name may become traitors to their faith.

The money that a man has he may lose. It flies away from him, perhaps when he needs it most. A man's reputation may be sacrificed in a moment of ill-considered action. The people who are prone to fall on their knees when success is with us, may be the first to throw the stone of malice when failure settles its cloud upon our head.

The one absolutely unselfish friend that man can have in this selfish world, the one that never deserts him, the one that never proves ungrateful or treacherous, is his dog. A man's dog stands by him in prosperity and poverty, in health and in sickness. He will sleep on the cold ground, where the wint'ry winds blow and the snow drives fiercely, if only he may be near his master's side. He will kiss the hand that has no food to offer; he will lick the wounds and sores that come in encounters with the roughness of the world. He guards the sleep of his pauper master as if he were a prince.

When all other friends desert, he remains. When riches take wings, and reputation falls to pieces, he is as constant in his love as the sun in its journey through the heavens.

If fortune drives his master forth an outcast in the world, friendless and homeless, the faithful dog asks no higher privilege than that of accompanying him, to guard him against danger, to fight against his enemies. And when the last scene of all comes, and death takes his master in its embrace and his body is laid away in the cold ground, no matter if all other friends pursue their way, there by the graveside will the noble dog be found, his head between his paws, his eyes sad, but open in alert watchfulness, faithful and true even in death.

Argument before a jury

HELEN HUNT JACKSON (1830–1885)

NEIGHBOR and friend of Emily Dickinson, Mrs. Jackson was anything but a recluse. A poet of reputation, she was also a crusader for justice to the Indians, and wrote *Ramona,* a highly successful novel, to make public material the government originally suppressed in a report she wrote. But it is her little "daisy" verse that is still quoted.

> All summer she scattered the daisy leaves;
>   They only mocked her as they fell.
> She said, "The daisy but deceives;
>   'He loves me not,' 'He loves me well,'
> One story no two daisies tell."
> Ah foolish heart, which waits and grieves,
>   Under the daisy's mocking spell.
>   *The Sign of the Daisy*

JAMES ABRAM GARFIELD (1831–1881)

THE twentieth President, who was assassinated before he really had a chance to show his caliber in high office, by his charm and felicity of speech became an early example of the "self-made American" who could prove that poverty does not necessarily beget crudity. Farm-born and poorly schooled, he nevertheless graduated from Williams College, was admitted to the Ohio bar and became a teacher of ancient languages and literature before going into politics. Fifty years after his death, his individuality was emphasized by publication and wide readership of his correspondence.

1. If wrinkles must be written upon our brows, let them not be written upon the heart. The spirit should not grow old.

2. Commerce links all mankind in one common brotherhood of mutual dependence and interests.

3. All free governments are managed by the combined wisdom and folly of the people.

4. A pound of pluck is worth a ton of luck.

5. In the long, fierce struggle for freedom of opinion, the press, like the Church, counted its martyrs by thousands.

6. I believe in God, and I trust myself in His hands.

FRANKLIN BENJAMIN SANBORN (1831–1917)

THIS New Hampshire author and philanthropist, who after a Harvard education made his career in Massachusetts, chose to express his own ideas through biographies of friends —among others, notably Alcott, Channing, Hawthorne, Emerson, Thoreau.

1. Dante might choose his home in all the wide, beautiful world; but to be out of the streets of Florence was exile to him. Socrates never cared to go beyond the bounds of Athens. The great universal heart welcomes the city as a natural growth of the eternal forces.

2. The careful reader of a few good newspapers can learn more in a year than most scholars do in their great libraries.

LOUISA MAY ALCOTT (1832–1888)

THE moralistic and idealistic author of *Little Women* won distinction in many fields. She gave more attention to prose than to poetry, but when she is quoted, the rhymed words linger in memory.

1. A little kingdom I possess,
     Where thoughts and feelings dwell;
And very hard the task I find
     Of governing it well.

.   .   .   .

I do not ask for any crown
     But that which all may win;

Nor try to conquer any world
  Except the one within. . . .

My Kingdom

2. For such as he there is no death;—
  His life the eternal life commands;
  Above man's aims his nature rose.
  The wisdom of a just content
  Made one small spot a continent,
  And turned to poetry Life's prose.

Thoreau's Flute

3. To smooth the rough and thorny way
   Where other feet begin to tread;
  To feed some hungry soul each day
   With sympathy's sustaining bread.

My Prayer

4. A child her wayward pencil drew
   On margins of her book:
  Garlands of flowers, dancing elves,
   Bird, butterfly and brook.
  Lessons undone, and play forgot,
   Seeking with hand and heart
  The teacher whom she learned to love
   Before she knew 'twas Art.

    . . . .

Death, the stern sculptor, with a touch
   No earthly power can stay,
Changes to marble in an hour
   The beautiful, pale clay.

Our Madonna

ELIZABETH AKERS ALLEN (1832–1911)

PUBLICATION in the *Saturday Evening Post* in June 1860, of a long poem, "Rock Me to Sleep," marked the first recognition of a popular and enduring poet who signed her name "Florence Percy."

1. Backward, turn backward, O Time, in your flight,
   Make me a child again just for tonight!

   .　　.　　.　　.

   Backward, flow backward, O tide of the years!
   I am so weary of toil and of tears—
   Toil without recompense, tears all in vain—
   Take them and give me my childhood again!

   .　　.　　.　　.

   Over my heart in the days that have flown,
   No love like mother-love ever has shone;
   No other worship abides and endures,
   Faithful, unselfish and patient, like yours.

                                    Rock Me to Sleep

2.　　　Unremembered and afar
   I watched you as I watched a star,
   Through darkness struggling into view,
   And loved you better than you knew.

                                    Left Behind

3. Carve not upon a stone when I am dead
        The praises which remorseful mourners give
   To women's graves—a tardy recompense—
        But speak them while I live.

                                    Till Death

4. Blush, happy maiden, when you feel
   The lips which press love's glowing seal;
   But as the slow years darklier roll,
   Grown wiser, the experienced soul
   Will own as dearer far than they
   The lips which kiss the tears away.

                                    Kisses

JOEL BENTON (1832–1911)

THE warm memory of Lincoln, and public feeling about him after his assassination, inspired a minor poet to a great tribute.

Some opulent force of genius, soul and race,
  Some deep life-current from far centuries,
Flowed to his mind and lighted his sad eyes,
  And gave his name, among great names, high place.
                                    LINCOLN—Another Washington

HENRY CLAY WORK (1832–1884)

HARDLY a poet in the traditional sense, but a composer of catchy doggerel, Work probably made the South angrier in the Civil War than any other northern individual with his "Marching Through Georgia." To "elocutionists" he bequeathed a tear-jerking recitation.

1. Bring the good old bugle, boys! We'll sing another song;
   Sing it with a spirit that will start the world along,
   Sing it as we used to sing it—fifty thousand strong,
   As we were marching through Georgia.
                                    Marching Through Georgia

2. Father, dear father, come home with me now,
   The clock in the belfry strikes one.
   You said you were coming right home from the shop
   As soon as your day's work was done.
                                    Come Home, Father

ROBERT GREEN INGERSOLL (1833–1899)

KNOWN principally as a man who made his agnosticism a profession, Ingersoll nevertheless was a polished, charming and gentle scholar and author. Forsaking law practice to write and talk on his beliefs he won admiration for his declamatory skill even from his critics.

1. Anger blows out the lamp of the mind. In the examination of a great and important question, everyone should be serene, slow-pulsed and calm.

2. The inspiration of the Bible depends upon the ignorance of the gentleman who reads it.

3. If I owe Smith ten dollars, and God forgives me, that doesn't pay Smith.

4. A mule has neither pride of ancestry nor hope of posterity.

5. Our hope of immortality does not come from any religion, but nearly all religions come from hope.

6. There is but one blasphemy, and that is injustice.

7. Insolence is not logic; epithets are the arguments of malice.

8. If I go to heaven, I want to take my reason with me.

9. I belong to the Great Church which holds the wilderness within its starlit aisles; that claims the great and good of every race and clime; that finds with joy the grain of gold in every creed, and floods with light and love the germs of good in every soul.

10. Life is a narrow vale between the cold and barren peaks of two eternities. We strive in vain to look beyond the heights. We cry aloud—and the only answer is the echo of our wailing cry. From the voiceless lips of the unreplying dead there comes no word. But in the night of Death Hope sees a star and listening Love can hear the rustling of a wing.

At his Brother's Grave, 1879

11. I am the inferior of any man whose rights I trample under foot. Men are not superior by reason of the accidents of race or color. They are superior who have the best heart—the best brain.

12. We, too, have our religion, and it is this: Help for the living, hope for the dead.

13. An honest God is the noblest work of man.

14. . . . I would rather have been a French peasant and worn wooden shoes. I would rather have lived in a hut with a vine growing over the door and the grapes growing purple in the kisses of the August sun. I would rather have been that poor peasant with my loving wife by my side, knitting as the day died out of the sky, with my children upon my knee and their arms about me. I would rather have been that man and gone down to the tongueless silence of the dreamless dust than to have been

that imperial personation of force and murder known as Napoleon the Great. And so I would ten thousand times.

After visiting the tomb of Napoleon

CHARLES FARRAR BROWNE (ARTEMUS WARD) (1834–1867)

BORN in Maine, Browne under his pseudonym quickly became famous for his native "sayings" with their peculiar spelling. In his brief life he established a reputation both as writer and homespun lecturer.

1. My pollertics, like my religion, being of an exceedin' accommodatin' character.

2. The fack can't be no longer disgised that a Krysis is onto us.

3. I am not a politician, but my other habits are good.

4. The prevailin' weakness of most public men is to Slop over. G. Washington . . . never slopt over!

5. I can't sing. As a singist I am not a success. I am saddest when I sing. So are those who hear me. They are sadder even than I am.

6. Did you ever have the measels, and if so, how many?

The Census

7. Let us all be happy and live within our means, even if we have to borrer the money to do it with. *Natural History*

8. The sun has a right to "set" where it wants to, and so, I may add, has a hen. *A Mormon Romance*

9. They cherish his mem'ry, and them as sell picturs of his birth-place, etc., make it prof'tible cherishin' it.

At the Tomb of Shakespeare

CHARLES W. ELIOT (1834–1926)

THIS famous president of Harvard, in forty years after his appointment as president at the age of thirty-five, changed it from a small college with affiliated graduate schools into its form as a great modern university. He searched after the ringing or quotable phrase, but produced a minor masterpiece when President Woodrow Wilson invited him to write inscriptions for the east and west pavilions of the Washington, D.C. Post Office, then edited them.

1. Carrier of news and knowledge
   Instrument of trade and commerce
   Promoter of mutual acquaintance
   Among men and nations and hence
   Of peace and good will.

   .　　.　　.　　.

2. Carrier of news and knowledge
   Messenger of friendship
   Consoler of the lonely
   Servant of the scattered family
   Enlarger of the public life.

President Wilson edited the lines to read as follows:

Carrier of news and knowledge
Instrument of trade and
Promoter of mutual acquaintance
Of peace and good will
Among men and nations.

.　　.　　.　　.

Messenger of sympathy and love
Servant of parted friends
Consoler of the lonely
Bond of the scattered family
Enlarger of the common life.

THOMAS BRIGHAM BISHOP
(1835–1905)

HERE was another songwriter inspired by the events of the Civil War period, who wrote what was to become a marching song of Union troops, a memorial to John Brown, leader of the fight at Harper's Ferry, and the immediate inspiration of Mrs. Howe's *Battle Hymn.*

John Brown's body lies a-mouldering in the grave,
His soul goes marching on.

John Brown's Body

PHILLIPS BROOKS (1835–1893)

THE Christmas hymn, "O Little Town of Bethlehem!", promises to be the most enduring monument to this scholarly minister, who became rector of famed Trinity Church in Boston and later was consecrated bishop of Massachusetts. He was, however, a man of many unusual talents, whose sincerity and fine oratorical skill left a wealth of expressions that seem as fresh today as when he spoke them.

1. A prayer, in its simplest definition, is merely a wish turned heavenward.

2. The truest help we can render an afflicted man is not to take his burden from him, but to call out his best energy, that he may be able to bear the burden.

3. Do not pray for easy lives. Pray to be stronger men! Do not pray for tasks equal to your powers. Pray for powers equal to your tasks.

4. Life comes before literature, as the material always comes before the work. The hills are full of marble before the world blooms with statues.

5. Men everywhere are trying to be safe by stifling life; by living just as low as possible. . . . The Bible comes glowing with protest. "Not so," it says. "Only by the fullness of life does safety come." . . . It is a noble assertion. The whole Bible, from its first page to its last, is full of the assertion of the fundamental necessity of vitality; that the first thing which a man needs in order to live well, is to live.

6. O little town of Bethlehem,
    How still we see thee lie;

> Above thy deep and dreamless sleep
>   The silent stars go by.
>
> Yet in thy dark streets shineth
>   The everlasting light;
> The hopes and fears of all the years
>   Are met in thee tonight.
>
> *O Little Town of Bethlehem*

7. Tomb, thou shalt hold Him no longer;
        Death is strong, but Life is stronger;
    Stronger than the dark, the light;
        Stronger than the wrong, the right;
    Faith and Hope triumphant say
        Christ will rise on Easter Day

An Easter Carol

SAMUEL LANGHORNE CLEMENS (MARK TWAIN) (1835–1910)

THIS journalist, lecturer, novelist and writer of travel books—all bearing the stamp of satiric genius —represents a unique epoch of American writing in himself. In none of the fields which he preempted with his skill, in a long career that began with success in his twenties, was Mark Twain quite like anyone else. Both his works and his experiences are far too broad to summarize here, but Mark Twain's place in American letters is secure and biographers still find him and his writings a rich source for their work.

1. When angry, count four! when very angry, swear.

2. It were not best that we should all think alike; it is difference of opinion that makes horse-races.

3. Adam and Eve had many advantages, but the principal one was that they escaped teething.

4. Training is everything. The peach was once a bitter almond; cauliflower is nothing but cabbage with a college education.

1–4: Pudd'nhead Wilson

5. Noise proves nothing. Often a hen who has merely laid an egg cackles as if she had laid an asteroid.

6. Persons attempting to find a motive in this narrative will be prosecuted; persons attempting to find a moral in it will be banished; persons attempting to find a plot in it will be shot.

7. Hain't we got all the fools in town on our side? And ain't that a big enough majority in any town?

8. Get your facts first, and then you can distort 'em as much as you please.

9. An experienced, industrious, ambitious, and often quite picturesque liar.   *6–9: The Adventures of Huckleberry Finn*

10. There are times when one would like to hang the whole human race, and finish the farce.

11. Modesty antedates clothes and will be resumed when clothes are no more.

12. Modesty died when clothes were born.

13. Modesty died when false modesty was born.

14. Man is the Only Animal that blushes. Or needs to.

Following the Equator

15. Fleas can be taught nearly everything that a Congressman can.

16. He is now fast rising from affluence to poverty.

Henry Beecher Ward's Farm

17. There are two times in a man's life when he should not speculate: when he can't afford it, and when he can.

18. All you need in this life is ignorance and confidence, and then Success is sure.   [*1887*]

19. This poor little one-horse town.   *The Undertaker's Chat*

20. Tell the truth or trump—but get the trick.

21. Everybody talks about the weather but nobody does anything about it.   *Attributed to Twain*

22. They spell it Vinci and pronounce it Vinchy; foreigners always spell better than they pronounce.   *The Innocents Abroad*

23. A classic is something that everybody wants to have read and nobody wants to read.

24. Work consists of whatever a body is *obliged* to do. . . . Play consists of whatever a body is not obliged to do.

The Adventures of Tom Sawyer

25. If you pick up a starving dog and make him prosperous, he will not bite you. This is the principal difference between a dog and a man.

26. The report of my death was an exaggeration.

Cable from Europe to the Associated Press

27. I was gratified to be able to answer promptly, and I did. I said I didn't know. *Life on the Mississippi*

28. War talk by a man who has been in a war is always interesting; whereas moon talk by a poet who has not been in the moon is likely to be dull. *Ibid.*

29. There is a sumptuous variety about the New England weather that compels the stranger's admiration—and regret. The weather is always doing something there; always attending strictly to business; always getting up new designs and trying them on people to see how they will go. But it gets through more business in spring than in any other season. In the spring I have counted one hundred and thirty-six different kinds of weather inside of four-and-twenty hours. *New England Weather*

30. Warm summer sun, shine kindly here;
Warm southern wind, blow softly here;
Green sod above, lie light, lie light—
Good-night, dear heart, good-night, good-night.

On the Tombstone of Susan Clemens

THEODORE TILTON (1835–1907)

THIS journalist, novelist and poet, and one-time popular lecturer, is remembered occasionally for two things: the poem from which this quotation is taken, and his suit against Henry Ward Beecher for alleged adultery with Mrs. Tilton— a trial that ended in a hung jury.

Once in Persia reigned a king,
Who upon his signet ring
Graved a maxim true and wise,
Which if held before the eyes
Gave him counsel at a glance

Fit for every change and chance;
Solemn words, and these are they:
"Even this shall pass away."

Even This Shall Pass Away

THOMAS BAILEY ALDRICH (1836–1907)

ALDRICH accomplished the impossible (in his generation): an outsider in Boston, he reached the peak of literary heights as editor of the *Atlantic Monthly,* from 1881 to 1890. Born in New Hampshire, with no recorded university background, he lived his first twenty-nine years in Portsmouth, New Orleans and New York. He had some success in all the literary fields, including playwrighting, but light verse and occasional satires were his forte.

1. It was very pleasant to me to get a letter from you the other day. Perhaps I should have found it pleasanter if I had been able to decipher it. I don't think that I mastered anything beyond the date (which I knew) and the signature (which I guessed at). There's a singular and a perpetual charm in a letter of yours; it never grows old, it never loses its novelty. . . . Other letters are read and thrown away and forgotten, but yours are kept forever —unread. One of them will last a reasonable man a lifetime.

Letter to Professor Edward S. Morse

2. What is lovely never dies,
    But passes into other loveliness,
  Star-dust, or sea-foam, flower or winged air.

A Shadow of the Night

3. So precious life is! Even to the old
    The hours are as a miser's coins!

Broken Music

4. You do poets and their song
  A grievous wrong,
  If your soul does not bring

To their high imagining
As much beauty as they sing.

Appreciation

5. When were December and May
    known to be happy together?

Thalia

6. Some weep because they part
And languish broken-hearted,
And others—O my heart!—
Because they never parted!

The Difference

7. When to soft Sleep we give ourselves away,
    And in a dream as in a fairy bark
Drift on and on through enchanted dark
    To purple daybreak—little thought we pay
To that sweet bitter world we know by day.

Sleep

8. They fail, and they alone, who have not striven.

"Enamored Architect of Airy Rhyme"

9. I like not lady-slippers,
    Nor yet the sweet-pea blossoms,
Nor yet the flaky roses,
    Red or white as snow:
I like the chaliced lilies,
    The gorgeous tiger-lilies,
That in our garden grow.

Tiger Lilies

10. October turned my maple's leaves to gold;
    The most are gone now; here and there one lingers;
Soon these will slip from out the twig's weak hold,
    Like coins between a dying miser's fingers.

Maple Leaves

11. Night is a stealthy, evil Raven,
    Wrapt to the eyes in his black wings.

Day and Night

12. What probing deep
Has ever solved the mysteries of sleep?

Human Ignorance

JOHN BURROUGHS (1837-1921)

ONE of the best known, if not the greatest, naturalist of his day, this self-taught and self-trained son of an upstate New York farmer had, at the age of thirty, already been a newspaper reporter, bank examiner, treasury clerk, and author of *Walt Whitman, Poet and Person*. Settling himself on a fruit farm, he devoted his time to agriculture and letters. Often compared with Thoreau, he lived far longer and achieved greater fame in his lifetime, winning from his friends the loving and descriptive title, "The Sage of Slabsides."

1. I was born with a chronic anxiety about the weather.

2. Literature is an investment of genius which pays dividends to all subsequent times.

3. It is always easier to believe than to deny. Our minds are naturally affirmative.

4. Time does not become sacred to us until we have lived it.

5. Nature teaches us more than she preaches. There are no sermons in stones. It is easier to get a spark out of a stone than a moral.

6. I go to books and to nature as the bee goes to a flower, for a nectar that I can make into my own honey.

7. Life is a struggle, but not a warfare.

8. The tendinous part of the mind, so to speak, is more developed in winter; the fleshy, in summer. I should say winter has given the bone and sinew to literature, summer the tissues and blood.

9. Serene, I fold my hands and wait,
     Nor care for wind, or tide, or sea;
   I rave no more 'gainst Time or Fate,
     For lo! my own shall come to me.

. . . .

   Nor time, nor space, nor deep, nor high,
     Can keep my own away from me.

Waiting

ANDREW CARNEGIE (1835–1919)

THIS son of a Scottish immigrant, who resigned his railroad job at the age of thirty to devote all of his time to building up investments he already had made in iron and steel development, amassed one of the greatest individual fortunes made by an American businessman. He established another record by giving away some $350 millions for public benefits and endowments. In 1889 he expressed a trenchant thought in an essay, *The Gospel of Wealth*.

Surplus wealth is a sacred trust which its possessor is bound to administer in his lifetime for the good of the community.

GROVER CLEVELAND (1837–1908)

THIS twenty-second President, son of a New Jersey preacher, was elected after an energetic campaign for "clean government." His fight against "machine politics" (including the activities of Tammany Hall), made him as notable for reform as some other Presidents have been for their leadership in crises. His political precepts are surely as true today as when he formulated them.

1. Public officers are the servants and agents of the people, to execute laws which the people have made and within the limits of a constitution which they have established.

2. Honor lies in honest toil.

3. Party honesty is partly expediency.

4. A truly American sentiment recognizes the dignity of labor.

5. Your every voter, as surely as your chief magistrate, exercises a public trust.   *First Inaugural Address*

6. The so-called debtor class . . . are not dishonest because they are in debt.

7. When more of the people's sustenance is exacted through the form of taxation than is necessary to meet the just obligations of the Government and expenses of its economical administra-

tion, such taxation becomes ruthless extortion and a violation of the fundamental principles of a free Government.

Second Annual Message, 1886

8. The lessons of paternalism ought to be unlearned and the better lesson taught that while the people should patriotically and cheerfully support their Government, its functions do not include the support of the people. *Second Inaugural Address*

WILLIAM DEAN HOWELLS (1837–1920)

THIS author, editor and critic, whose "education" consisted of a printer's apprenticeship in boyhood, became editor of the *Ohio State Journal* at the age of twenty-one. Death came to him in the twentieth year of his writing the "Easy Chair" column for *Harper's Magazine*. In those two decades, which encompassed fifteen years of editing the *Atlantic Monthly*, Howells produced a shelf of books which placed him in the first rank of American literary figures.

1. The Bostonian who leaves Boston ought to be condemned to perpetual exile. *The Rise of Silas Lapham*

2. The book which you read from a sense of duty, or because for any reason you must, does not commonly make friends with you. It may happen that it will yield you an unexpected delight, but this will be in its own unentreated way and in spite of your good intentions.

3. I am not sorry for having wrought in common, crude material so much; that is the right American stuff; and perhaps hereafter, when my din is done, if any one is curious to know what that noise was, it will be found to have proceeded from a small insect which was scraping about on the surface of our life and trying to get into its meaning for the sake of the other insects larger or smaller. That is, such has been my unconscious work; consciously, I was always, and I still am, trying to fashion a piece of literature out of the life next at hand.

Letter to Charles E. Norton, 1903

HORACE PORTER (1837–1921)

AS soldier, statesman, diplomat, Porter won the usual distinctions. When ambassador to France, he displayed the patriotic sentiment that prompted him to return the body of John Paul Jones to the United States, at his own expense. To the field of quotations he made one great contribution—his definition of a political "mugwump."

A mugwump is a person educated beyond his intellect.

HENRY ADAMS (1838–1918)

THIS great-grandson of John Adams abandoned both traditional callings of his famous family—the law and politics—to specialize in writing history, a field in which he made his name famous. However, it was his own autobiography, *The Education of Henry Adams,* first printed privately in 1906 and published posthumously in 1918, that provided the source for the following great quotations.

1. Even in America, the Indian summer of life should be a little sunny and a little sad, like the season, and infinite in wealth and depth of tone—but never hustled.

2. Although the Senate is much given to admiring in its members a superiority less obvious or quite invisible to outsiders, one Senator seldom proclaims his own inferiority to another, and still more seldom likes to be told of it.

3. No one means all he says, and yet very few say all they mean, for words are slippery and thought is viscous.

4. Nothing in education is so astonishing as the amount of ignorance it accumulates in the form of inert facts.

5. All experience is an arch, to build upon.

6. One friend in a lifetime is much; two are many; three are hardly possible. Friendship needs a certain parallelism of life, a community of thought, a rivalry of aim.

7. Friends are born, not made.

8. Chaos often breeds life, when order breeds habit.

9. The difference is slight, to the influence of an author, whether he is read by five hundred readers, or by five hundred thousand; if he can select the five hundred, he reaches the five hundred thousand.

10. A teacher affects eternity; he can never tell where his influence stops.

11. The newspaper-man is, more than most men, a double personality; and his person feels best satisfied in its double instincts when writing in one sense and thinking in another.

12. Accident counts much for companionship as in marriage.

13. Knowledge of human nature is the beginning and end of political education.

14. Practical politics consists in ignoring the facts.

15. Power is poison. Its effects on Presidents had always been tragic, chiefly as an almost insane excitement at first, and a worse reaction afterwards; but also because no mind is so well balanced as to bear the strain of seizing unlimited force without habit or knowledge of it; and finding it disputed with him by hungry packs of wolves and hounds whose lives depend on snatching the carrion.

16. We combat obstacles in order to get repose, and, when got, the repose is insupportable.

17. Simplicity is the most deceitful mistress that ever betrayed a man.

18. Women have, commonly, a very positive moral sense; that which they will, is right; that which they reject, is wrong; and their will, in most cases, ends by settling the moral.

19. Young men have a passion for regarding their elders as senile.

GEORGE DEWEY (1838–1917)

AT dawn on May 2, 1898, this American admiral led the Asiatic Squadron to an attack on a Spanish fleet in Manila Bay—the first engagement between American and foreign warships since the War of

1812. Facing this decision—not knowing that within a few hours he would win a victory that destroyed the Spaniards at a cost of only eight wounded Americans, Dewey turned to his gunnery officer and gave a laconic, but historic order.

You may fire when you are ready, Gridley.

JOHN HAY (1838–1905)

IN the history books, Hay is praised as a diplomat and statesman. He was Secretary of State under Mc-Kinley and Roosevelt, author of the Open Door policy for China, and negotiator of other important treaties. But half a century after his death, his enduring personal words are those of a poet—poetry was his lifetime avocation.

1. The King will be well if he sleeps one night
   In the shirt of a happy man.

   The Enchanted Shirt

2. Good luck is the gayest of all gay girls,
   Long in one place she will not stay,
   Back from your brow she strokes the curls,
   Kisses you quick and flies away.
   But Madame Bad Luck soberly comes

   .   .   .   .

   And sits by your bed, and brings her knitting.

   Good Luck and Bad

There are three species of creatures who when they seem
   coming are going,
When they seem going they come: Diplomats, women and
   crabs.

   .   .   .   .

True luck consists not in holding the best of the cards at
   the table:
Luckiest he who knows just when to rise and go home.

   Distichs

HEZEKIAH BUTTERWORTH
(1839–1905)

THE editor who made a notable success of the *Youth's Companion,* excelled as a writer of juvenile stories. He also wrote several volumes of verse, from which two gems often are remembered.

1. Each loss has its compensation,
   There is healing for every pain,
   But the bird with a broken pinion
   Never soars so high again.

   The Bird With a Broken Wing

2. One taper lights a thousand,
   Yet it shines as it has shone;
   And the humblest light may kindle
   A brighter than its own.

   The Taper

FRANCIS PHARCELLUS CHURCH
(1839–1906)

A little girl named Virginia O'Hanlon was troubled in 1897 to hear from playmates a report that there really was no Santa Claus. Her father, to whom she took her problem, suggested she write to the *New York Sun,* whose editors certainly would know whether the report were true. Virginia did write to the *Sun.* Church, one of the editorial writers, replied to her with a column, entitled "Yes, Virginia, There Is a Santa Claus." His words have become a classic.

Virginia, your little friends are wrong. They have been affected by the skepticism of a skeptical age. They do not believe except they see. They think that nothing can be which is not comprehensible by their little minds. All minds, Virginia, whether they be men's or children's, are little. In this great universe of ours man is a mere insect, an ant, in his intellect, as compared with the boundless world about him, as measured by the intelligence capable of grasping the whole of truth and knowledge.

.   .   .   .

Not believe in Santa Claus? You might as well not believe in fairies.

No Santa Claus! Thank God, he lives, and he lives forever. A thousand years from now, Virginia, nay, ten times ten thousand years from now, he will continue to make glad the heart of childhood.

HENRY GEORGE (1839–1897)

OUT of personal experience with deep poverty, self-education in economics, and apparently a sincere public spirit, Henry George struggled into prominence with his single-tax theory in his controversial work *Progress and Poverty*. Though he achieved no important position personally, his theories became a matter of world-wide debate, and exerted influence on subsequent tax legislation.

1. Capital is the result of labor, and is used by labor to assist it in further production. Labor is the active and initial force, and labor is therefore the employer of capital.

2. That which is unjust can really profit no one; that which is just can really harm no one.

3. For as labor cannot produce without the use of land, the denial of the equal right to use of land is necessarily the denial of the right of labor to its own produce.

4. That amid our highest civilization men faint and die with want is not due to the niggardliness of nature, but to the injustice of man.

5. So long as all the increased wealth which modern progress brings goes but to build up great fortunes, to increase luxury, and make sharper the contrast between the House of Have and the House of Want, progress is not real and cannot be permanent.

6. The man who gives me employment, which I must have

or suffer, that man is my master, let me call him what I will.

7. The ideal social state is not that in which each gets an equal amount of wealth, but in which each gets in proportion to his contribution to the general stock.

(FRANCIS) BRET HARTE (1836–1902)

HUMORIST Bret Harte actually spent only a short part of his life in San Francisco, although he is known primarily as a "western" writer. These years did see his best work. Drifting westward from Albany, he prospected for gold, taught school and finally became clerk in the mint. The editorship of a paper occupied his energies until 1871, when he made his home in New York. The last part of his life was spent in London; nevertheless, for us his is the voice of the old West.

1. Which I wish to remark,
   And my language is plain,
   That for ways that are dark
   And for tricks that are vain,
   The heathen Chinee is peculiar.

Plain Language from Truthful James

2. But still, when the mists of Doubt prevail,
   And we lie becalmed by the shores of Age,
   We hear from the misty troubled shore
   The voice of the children gone before,
   Drawing the soul to its anchorage.

A Greyport Legend

3. Brief words, when actions wait, are well:
   The prompter's hand is on the bell;
   The coming heroes, lovers, kings,
   Are idly lounging in the wings;
   Behind the curtain's mystic fold
   The glowing future lies unrolled.

Speech at opening of the California Theatre, San Francisco, 1870

MADAME DE SALM (1840–?)

WHAT fun it would be to know something of Madame de Salm, an actress with this assumed name, the date of whose death is as much a mystery as her true identity. Her wit lives in one quotation.

Men who flatter them [women] do not know them; men who abuse them know them still less.

HENRY WATTERSON (1840–1921)

IN the days when newspapers reflected the tempestuous personalities of their editor-owners, and the daily journals of smaller cities often attracted international respect, "Marse" Henry Watterson was the czar and *genius domus* of the Louisville COURIER-JOURNAL. Typical of his fire—and his times—was his reply to a rebuke aimed at him for criticizing the Governor of Kentucky.

Things have come to a helluva pass
When a man can't cudgel his own jackass.

ROSSITER JOHNSON (1840–1931)

HIS career as editor of encyclopedias, the eighteen-volume collection "Little Classics," and the forty-volume "The World's Great Books" brought him great success, but Johnson found his personal creative outlet in verse, much of it dealing with the weather.

1. How it pours, pours, pours,
    In a never-ending sheet!
How it drives beneath the doors!
    How it soaks the passer's feet!

How it rattles on the shutter!
How it rumples up the lawn!
How 'twill sigh, and moan, and mutter,
From darkness until dawn!

The Rhyme of the Rain

2. O for a lodge in a garden of cucumbers!
O for an iceberg or two at control!
O for a vale which at mid-day the dew cumbers!
O for a pleasure trip up to the Pole!

Ninety-nine in the Shade

CHARLES E. WELLER (1840–1925)

WHEN typewriters were a new invention, and purchasers had to be instructed in how to master them, Weller invented a finger exercise. Still used by every learner, it is a perennial slogan.

Now is the time for all good men to come to the aid of their party.

OLIVER WENDELL HOLMES, JR. (1841–1935)

THE son of "The Autocrat of the Breakfast-Table" won distinction as a great liberal voice in the Supreme Court of the United States. The "Great Dissenter" was famous for his opinions written with the force and clarity of a legal genius. But Holmes' sense of humor complemented the more serious part of his nature. The first quotation is ascribed to him by friends, on the occasion of his passing a pretty girl on the street, when he was about eighty-five years of age.

1. O to be seventy again!
2. The riders in a race do not stop short when they reach the goal. There is a little finishing canter before coming to a standstill. There is time to hear the kind voice of friends and to say to one's

self: "The work is done." But just as one says that, the answer comes: "The race is over, but the work never is done while the power to work remains." The canter that brings you to a standstill need not be only coming to rest. It cannot be, while you still live. For to live is to function. That is all there is to living.

And so I end with a line from a Latin poet who uttered the message more than fifteen hundred years ago, "Death plucks my ear and says: Live—I am coming."

This is a complete transcript of Mr. Justice Holmes' response at the end of an hour-long, nation-wide tribute to him by national radio hook-up on his 90th birthday, March 7, 1931

CINCINNATUS HINER (JOAQUIN) MILLER (1841–1913)

MILLER, the Indiana boy with the classical name, travelled a long way to become Joaquin Miller, the costumed westerner and internationally famous writer of "Songs of the Sierra." The new personality was honestly come by, for Miller was an express-rider, gold miner, and sometime-resident with the Northwest Indians before he turned to the prosaic careers of editor and judge in Oregon.

1. That man who lives for self alone
   Lives for the meanest mortal known.

   Walker in Nicaragua

2. I do not question school or creed
   Of Christian, Protestant, or Priest;
   I only know that creeds to me
   Are but new names for mystery,
   That good is good from east to east.
   And more I do not know or need
   To know, to love my neighbor well.

   The Tale of the Tall Alcade

3. In men whom men condemn as ill
   I find so much of goodness still,

In men whom men pronounce divine
I find so much of sin and blot,
I do not dare to draw a line
Between the two, where God has not.

Byron

4. The bravest battle that ever was fought;
Shall I tell you where and when?
On the maps of the world you will find it not;
It was fought by the mothers of men.

The Bravest Battle

5. The biggest dog has been a pup.

William Brown of Oregon

6. Man's books are but man's alphabet,
Beyond and on his lessons lie—
The lessons of the violet,
The large gold letters of the sky.

.   .   .   .

The soul that feeds on books alone—
I count that soul exceeding small
That lives alone by book and creed,—
A soul that has not learned to read.

The Larger College [*Man's Books*]

EUGENE FITCH WARE (IRONQUILL)
(1841–1911)

ANOTHER poet who adopted a striking pen name, Ironquill seemingly had no eccentricities or mannerisms. His name is seldom noted in reference works and his life rarely sketched, but his poetry is often quoted for its felicity of expression.

1. Human hopes and human creeds
Have their root in human needs.

Rhymes of Ironquill

2. The charm of a love is its telling, the telling that goes with
   the giving;

The charm of a deed is its doing; the charm of a life is its
  living;
The soul of the thing is the thought; the charm of the act
  is the actor;
The soul of the fact is its truth, and the NOW is its principal factor.

The Now

3. Man builds no structure which outlives a book.

The Book

4. The farmer works the soil,
The agriculturist works the farmer.

The Kansas Bandit

AMBROSE BIERCE (1842–?)

BIERCE'S sardonic outlook on life prevented him from being considered a philosopher in the true sense. He may have missed greatness, but there is no question of his quotability. A brilliant editor and writer with early success first in San Francisco and then London, he later became a Washington correspondent. His savage satires on the foibles of the human race are classics of their kind. One wonders what satanic fate led the author of *The Devil's Dictionary* to Mexico in 1914, where he disappeared without further trace.

1. Woman would be more charming if one could fall into her arms without falling into her hands.

2. New York is cocaine, opium, hashish.

3. You are not permitted to kill a woman who has injured you, but nothing forbids you to reflect that she is growing older every minute. You are avenged 1440 times a day.

4. Self-denial is indulgence of a propensity to forego.

1–4: Epigrams

5. *Ability* is found mainly to consist in a high degree of solemnity.

Admiration: Our polite recognition of another's resemblance to ourselves.

Applause: The echo of a platitude.

Bore: A person who talks when you wish him to listen.

Conservative: A statesman who is enamored with the existing evils, as distinguished from the *Liberal,* who wishes to replace them with others.

Garter: An elastic band intended to keep a woman from coming out of her stockings and desolating the country.

Labor: One of the processes by which A acquires property for B.

Marriage: A community consisting of a master, a mistress, and two slaves, making in all, two.

Philosophy: A route of many roads leading from nowhere to nothing.   *The Devil's Dictionary*

6. Don't steal; thou'lt never thus compete successfully in business. Cheat.   *The Decalogue Revised*

THE BROTHERS JAMES

THE sons of Henry James, the Swedenborgian theologian and student of social problems, William and Henry James were major figures in the intellectual life of the nineteenth century. They had in common a broad culture and cosmopolitan outlook that brought to their accomplishments a universalism unusual in that era.

After both youths received a preliminary education in New York, they entered Harvard. There William earned a medical degree, the beginning of a lifelong association with the faculty. From 1872 he lectured on anatomy and physiology and, after 1880, taught in the departments of psychology and philosophy, where he became the acknowledged exponent of the new theory of knowledge called "Pragmatism."

Henry took a degree in law at the university, but with the encouragement of the Cambridge literary circle, which included Lowell, Norton and Howells, soon began to devote his energies to essays and fiction. Drawn irresistibly "back to the sources" this James, by the time he was thirty-four, had settled permanently in England. He became a British subject a year before his death. Some of his best-known works, including *The Ambassadors* explore the contrasts between European and American values.

WILLIAM JAMES (1842–1910)

1. It is well for the world that in most of us, by the age of thirty, the character has set like plaster, and will never soften again.

2. There is no more miserable human being than one in whom nothing is habitual but indecision.

3. No matter how full a reservoir of *maxims* one may possess, and no matter how good one's *sentiments* may be, if one have not taken advantage of every concrete opportunity to *act,* one's character may retain entirely unaffected for the better. With mere good intentions, hell is proverbially paved.

4. Keep the faculty of effort alive in you by a little gratuitous exercise each day. That is, be systematically ascetic or heroic in little unnecessary points, do every day or two something for no other reason than that you would rather not do it, so that when the hour of dire need draws nigh, it may find you not unnerved and untrained to stand the test.

5. The hell to be endured hereafter, of which theology tells, is no worse than the hell we make for ourselves in this world by habitually fashioning our characters in the wrong way.

6. We are not only gregarious animals, liking to be in sight of our fellows, but we have an innate propensity to get ourselves noticed, and noticed favorably, by our kind. No more fiendish punishment could be devised, were such a thing physically possible, than that one should be turned loose in society and remain absolutely unnoticed by all the members thereof.

7. In the practical as in the theoretic life, the man whose acquisitions *stick* is the man who is always achieving and advancing, whilst his neighbors, spending most of their time in relearning what they once knew but have forgotten, simply hold their own.

8. Genius, in truth, means little more than the faculty of perceiving in an unhabitual way.   *1–8: Principles of Psychology*

9. The deepest thing in our nature is . . . this dumb region

of the heart in which we dwell alone with our willingnesses and our unwillingnesses, our faiths and our fears.   *The Will to Believe*

10. Be not afraid of life. Believe that life *is* worth living, and your belief will help create the fact.   *Ibid.*

11. The whole drift of my education goes to persuade me that the world of our present consciousness is only one out of many worlds of consciousness that exist.

Varieties of Religious Experience

HENRY JAMES (1843–1916)

1. (*of Thoreau*) He was worse than provincial—he was parochial.

2. The very sign of its [New York's] energy is that it doesn't believe in itself; it fails to succeed, even at the cost of millions in persuading you that it does.

3. There are few hours in life more agreeable than the hour dedicated to the ceremony known as afternoon tea.

4. The time-honored bread-sauce of the happy ending.

5. There are few things more exciting to me . . . than a psychological reason.   *The Art of Fiction*

SIDNEY LANIER (1842–1881)

THIS Georgia musician and poet, with health shattered by wounds and imprisonment in the Civil War, in a few years mastered his chosen arts well. The year before his death saw publication of a book on the interrelation of music and poetry, composed of lectures he had been invited to deliver at Johns Hopkins University. This gemlike stanza comes from the loveliest of his works.

Through seas of dreams and seas of phantasies,
Through seas of solitudes and vacancies,

> And through my Self, the deepest of the seas,
> I strive to thee, Nirvana.

Nirvana

ARTHUR MACY (1842–1904)

MACY was no member of Boston's elite literary circle, but he had an ear for effect in the composition of poetry.

1. Cheers for the sailors that fought on the wave for it,
   Cheers for the soldiers that always were brave for it,
   Tears for the men that went down to the grave for it.
   Here comes the Flag!

Here Comes the Flag

2. Dear Omar, should you chance to meet
   Our Brother Somewhere in the Gloom,
   Pray give to Him a Message Sweet,
   For Brothers in the Tavern Room.
   He will not ask who 'tis that sends,
   For We were Friends.

Sit Closer, Friends: To the Papyrus Club, Boston

RUSSELL HERMAN CONWELL (1843–1925)

TRAINED as a lawyer, Conwell became a Baptist minister in 1879. In 1884 he opened Temple University and was appointed its first president. Aside from these distinctions he lectured for more than forty years. Undoubtedly his and his audiences' favorite was "Acres of Diamonds," which he gave some 6,000 times. Setting aside all proceeds from this lecture in a scholarship fund, Conwell estimated it financed the education of at least 10,000 young men. This accomplishment gives particular point to his famous quotation.

I ask not for a larger garden
But for finer seeds.

My Prayer

HUGH ANTOINE D'ARCY
(1843–1925)

D'ARCY'S one famous "tear-jerker" in verse, written in 1887, is often incorrectly called "The Face on the Barroom Floor." Somewhere tonight or any night, D'Arcy's work will be recited at a party by someone who probably never knew his name.

With chalk in hand the vagabond began
To sketch a face that well might buy the soul of any man.
Then he placed another lock upon the shapely head,
With a fearful shriek he leaped and fell across the picture
——dead!

The Face upon the Floor

JAMES HENRY MULLIGAN
(1844–1916)

AS poetry and philosophy matured in America, so did the development of robust song, not patterned after any European model, with the possible exception of the German student songs. Even here the similarities were in spirit rather than in rhythm. Mulligan was one of a score of writers who found inspiration in Kentucky.

The moonlight is the softest, in Kentucky,
Summer days come oftest, in Kentucky,
      Friendship is the strongest,
      Love's fires glow the longest,
      Yet a wrong is always wrongest,
            In Kentucky.

·   ·   ·   ·

> Songbirds are sweetest in Kentucky,
>> Thoroughbreds the fleetest, in Kentucky;
>> The mountains tower proudest,
>> Thunder peals the loudest,
>> The landscape is the grandest,
>> And politics the damnedest,
>>> In Kentucky.

In Kentucky

JOHN B. BOGART (1845–1921)

BOGART was a famous city editor of the New York *Sun,* from 1873 to 1900. In exasperation one day, he defined news—a definition which has been passed on to every cub reporter.

When a dog bites a man, that is not news, because it happens so often. But if a man bites a dog, that is news.

WILL CARLETON (1845–1912)

THIS Michigan-born writer made his success primarily with poems of rural life, for he wrote at a period when the city dwellers of an urbanized United States appreciated such nostalgia. In his best-known poem, Carleton gave us "Over the Hill to the Poor-House."

1. Thanksgiving-day, I fear,
   If one the solemn truth must touch,
   Is celebrated, not so much
   To thank the Lord for blessings o'er,
   As for the sake of getting more!

   Captain Young's Thanksgiving

2. If there's a heaven upon the earth, a fellow knows it when
   He's been away from home a week, and then gets back
   again.

   Goin' Home Today

3. He has seen old views and patients disappearing, one by
     one,
   He has learned that Death is master both of Science and
     Art.

The Country Doctor

4.   To appreciate heaven well
   'Tis good for a man to have some fifteen minutes of hell.

Gone With a Handsomer Man

5. Over the hill to the poor-house I'm trudgin' my weary way.

Over the Hill to the Poor-House

FIVE POETS

THE five writers following are grouped under one heading, not because of marked similarities in their work, but to illustrate the proliferating production of poetry, and the fact that appreciative audiences made a market for it. In their works most readers will discover the source of familiar words often recollected.

SARAH CHAUNCEY WOOLSEY (SUSAN COOLIDGE) (1835–1905)

The punctual tide draws up the bay,
With ripple of wave and hiss of spray.

On the Shore

JOHN BANISTER TABB (1845–1909)

1. A flash of harmless lightning,
       A mist of rainbow dyes,
   The burnished sunbeams brightening
       From flower to flower he flies.

Humming Bird

2. How many an acorn falls to die
    For one that makes a tree!
How many a heart must pass me by
    For one that cleaves to me!

Compensation

ALONZO B. BRAGDON (1847–1902)

Alas, how scant the sheaves for all the trouble,
    The toil, the pain, and the resolve sublime—
A few full ears; the rest but weeds and stubble,
    And withered wild-flowers plucked before their time.

The Old Campus

JOHN VANCE CHENEY (1848–1922)

1. I question not if thrushes sing,
    If roses load the air;
Beyond my heart I need not reach
    When all is summer there.

Love's World

2. Who drives the horses of the sun
    Shall lord it but a day;
Better the lowly deed were done,
    And kept the humble way.

. . . .

The happiest heart that ever beat
    Was in some quiet breast
That found the common daylight sweet,
    And left to Heaven the rest.

The Happiest Heart

FREDERICK LANGBRIDGE
(1849–1923)

Yield thy poor best, and muse not how or why,
Lest one day, seeing all about these spread
A mighty crowd and marvellously fed,
Thy heart break out into a bitter cry:
"I might have furnished, I, yea, even I,
The two small fishes and the barley bread."

.   .   .   .

Two men look out through the same bars;
One sees the mud, and one the stars.

A Cluster of Quiet Thoughts

THOMAS ALVA EDISON
(1847–1931)

THE genius of practical science, who seemed almost indefatigable, left in addition to his myriad inventions many proverbs.

1. Genius is one per cent inspiration and ninety-nine per cent perspiration.
2. I never did anything worth doing by accident, nor did any of my inventions come by accident; they came by work.

JOEL CHANDLER HARRIS
(1848–1908)

THIS Georgia-born writer became famous as a homespun philosopher, through the proverbs he put into the mouth of his character "Uncle Remus," who was introduced in a newspaper column and went on to be the subject of books. Harris' stories perfectly captured the dialect of the Georgia Negro of his time.

Lazy fokes' stummucks don't git tired.

Jay-bird don't rob his own nes'.

Licker talks mighty loud w'en it gits loose fum de jug.

Hungry rooster don't cackle w'en he fine a wum. . . .

Youk'n hide de fier, but w'at you gwine do wid de smoke?

Dogs don't bite at de front gate.

Watch out w'en youer gittin' all you want. Fattenin' hogs ain't in luck.

Ez soshubble ez a baskit er kittens.

WILLIAM HENRY THOMPSON
(1848–1918)

THE legend of southern chivalry and bravery in the Civil War was in its prime in 1888 when Thompson wrote with more emotion than historical accuracy an ode to the men in gray at Gettysburg.

Then, at the brief command of Lee,
Moved out that matchless infantry,
With Pickett leading grandly down,
To rush against the roaring crown
Of those dread heights of destiny.

The brave went down! Without disgrace
They leaped to Ruin's red embrace;
They only heard Fame's thunders wake,
And saw the dazzling sunburst break
In smiles on Glory's bloody face!

Fold up the banners! Smelt the guns!
Love rules. Her gentler purpose runs;
A mighty mother turns in tears
The pages of her battle years,
Lamenting all her fallen sons!

The High Tide at Gettysburg

JAMES LANE ALLEN (1849–1925)

ALTHOUGH Allen's romantic novel, *A Kentucky Cardinal,* was published in 1894, it still finds interested readers. The author, a native of Kentucky, who personified the movement of writers and artists developing on newer American soil, made a financial as well as artistic success with his books. In 1935 a biographer, G. C. Knight, wrote of Allen and "the genteel tradition."

Good friend, around these hearthstones speak no evil word of any creature.

.　　.　　.　　.

The finest music in the room is that which streams out to the ear of the spirit in many an exquisite strain from the little shelf of books on the opposite wall. Every volume there is an instrument which some melodist in the mind created and set vibrating with music.

.　　.　　.　　.

The birds are moulting. If man could only moult also—his mind once a year its errors, his heart once a year its useless passions.

.　　.　　.　　.

I have yet to encounter that common myth of weak men, an insurmountable barrier.

A Kentucky Cardinal

EMMA LAZARUS (1849–1887)

IN her relatively short life, Miss Lazarus—born and privately educated in New York—spanned a field of interest from writing distinguished poetry and translating Heine's poems and ballads, to active work on behalf of Russian Jewish refugees in America. But her "immortality" rests on a sonnet, "The New Colossus," dedicated to the Statue of Liberty, written in 1886 and is inscribed on its pedestal.

Give me your tired, your poor,
Your huddled masses yearning to breathe free,
The wretched refuse of your teeming shore,
Send these, the homeless, tempest-tossed, to me:
I lift my lamp beside the golden door.

Not like the brazen giant of Greek fame,
With conquering limbs astride from land to land;
Here at our sea-washed, sunset gates shall stand
A mighty woman with a torch, whose flame
Is the imprisoned lightning, and her name
    Mother of exiles.

The New Colossus

JAMES WHITCOMB RILEY
(1849–1916)

THE "Hoosier poet," whose nickname bespoke his Indiana origin, lived to enjoy international fame as a result of his mastery of humorous poetry in Middle Western dialect. His honors include the award of the gold medal of the National Institute of Arts and Letters. His best-known work is "Little Orphant Annie," but many others boast the humor and sentiment that have endeared them to generations.

1. The ripest peach is highest on the tree.

The Ripest Peach

2. And all us other children, when the supper things is done,
We set around the kitchen fire an' has the mostest fun
A-list'nin' to the witch tales 'at Annie tells about,
An' the gobble-uns 'at git you
    Ef you / Don't / Watch / Out!

Little Orphant Annie

3. But Heaven holds all for which you sigh.—
    There! little girl, don't cry!

A Life-Lesson

4. As one who cons at evening o'er an album all alone

And muses on the faces of the friends that he has known,
So I turn the leaves of Fancy, till in shadowy design
I find the smiling features of an old sweetheart of mine.
                                        An Old Sweetheart of Mine

5. "God bless us every one!" prayed Tiny Tim.
                                        God Bless Us Every One

6. O, it sets my heart a clickin' like the tickin' of a clock,
   When the frost is on the punkin and the fodder's in the
   shock.
                                        "When the Frost Is on the Punkin"

EUGENE FIELD (1850–1895)

AS a newspaperman in his native St. Louis, Denver and Chicago, who found his forte as a columnist, Field paved the way for a host of successful light poet-philosophers in this career. Few, however, have yet produced as appealing works as Field's evergreen "Wynken, Blynken and Nod" or "Little Boy Blue," or "The Sugar-Plum Tree."

1. Some statesmen go to Congress and some to jail. It is the same thing, after all.

2. All human joys are swift of wing,
      For heaven doth so allot it;
   That when you get an easy thing,
      You find you haven't got it.
                                        Ways of Life

3. Wynken, Blynken, and Nod one night
      Sailed off in a wooden shoe—
   Sailed on a river of crystal light
      Into a sea of dew.
                                        Wynken, Blynken and Nod

4. When one's all right, he's prone to spite
      The doctor's peaceful mission;
   But when he's sick, it's loud and quick
      He bawls for a physician.
                                        Doctors

5. When I demanded of my friend what viands he preferred,
   He quoth: "A large cold bottle, and a small hot bird!"
                                        The Bottle and the Bird
6. Have you ever heard of the Sugar-Plum Tree?
      'Tis a marvel of great renown!
   It blooms on the shore of the Lollipop Sea
      In the garden of Shut-Eye Town.
                                        The Sugar-Plum Tree
7. The little toy dog is covered with dust,
      But sturdy and stanch he stands;
   And the little toy soldier is red with rust,
      and his musket moulds in his hands;
   Time was when the little toy dog was new,
      and the soldier was passing fair;
   And that was the time when our Little Boy Blue
      Kissed them and put them there.
                                        Little Boy Blue

WILLIAM HAMILTON GIBSON (1850–1896)

TO a handful of art collectors, Gibson's delicately contrived sketches for illustrations of agricultural and nature publications are well known. The same poetical response to nature is found in his writings.

1. Oh, the lovely fickleness of an April day.
2. The wind moans, like a long wail from some despairing soul shut out in the awful storm.

HENRY CABOT LODGE (1850–1924)

LIKE his contemporary, Henry Adams, the first Senator Lodge left Harvard with doctorates in law and philosophy. His accomplishments as an editor, author and biographer alone would have distinguished him, but in addition he was Senator from Massachusetts from 1893 to 1924. The subjects of his biographies included George Cabot, his great-grandfather; Alexander Hamilton, Daniel Webster and George Washington. Despite his own conservatism, he was an intimate friend of the ebullient Theodore Roosevelt.

1. New England has a harsh climate, a barren soil, a rough and stormy coast, and yet we love it, even with a love passing that of dwellers in more favored regions.   *Speech, 1884*

2. Let every man honor and love the land of his birth and the race from which he springs and keep their memory green. It is a pious and honorable duty. But let us have done with British-Americans and Irish-Americans and German-Americans, and so on, and all be Americans. . . . If a man is going to be an American at all let him be so without any qualifying adjectives; and if he is going to be something else, let him drop the word American from his personal description.   *Speech, 1888*

3. There was no hour down to the end when he would not turn aside from everything else to preach the doctrine of Americanism, of the principles and the faith upon which American government rested, and which all true Americans should wear in their heart of hearts. He was a great patriot, a great man; above all, a great American. His country was the ruling, mastering passion of his life from the beginning even unto the end.

Eulogy for Theodore Roosevelt, before Congress, February 9, 1919

ROSE HARTWICK THORPE
(1850–1939)

ABOUT some writings there is a mystery (which this editor will not try to fathom), that makes them live for no apparent reason except the catchy twist of a line. One poem has drawn an unexpected popularity; Miss Thorpe's rather long and often dull masterwork, which on one occasion was stretched out to make the plot of a motion picture. This excerpt from it might be described as good Longfellowese.

Long, long years I've rung the curfew from that gloomy,
   shadowed tower;
Every evening, just at sunset, it has told the twilight hour;
I have done my duty ever, tried to do it just and right,
Now I'm old I will not falter—curfew it must ring tonight.

Curfew Must Not Ring Tonight

CHANGING
ORDER

DANIEL SCOTT LAMONT
(1851–1905)

LAMONT advanced from private secretary to Cleveland in the president's first Administration, to Secretary of War in the second. His ideals reflected those of his chief, ideals Lamont put into words.

Public office is a public trust.

EDWIN MARKHAM (1852–1940)

BORN in Oregon, later a California resident, Markham sprang into national prominence as a poet with publication of "The Man With the Hoe" when he was forty-seven years old. Thereafter, his reputation was secure and he lived long to enjoy it. His "Lincoln, the Man of the People," was published in 1901.

1. The crest and crowning of all good,
      Life's final star, is Brotherhood.

Brotherhood

2. Bowed by the weight of centuries he leans
    Upon his hoe and gazes on the ground,
    The emptiness of ages in his face,
    And on his back the burden of the world.

The Man With the Hoe

3. Here was a man to hold against the world,
    A man to match the mountains and the sea.

.   .   .   .

    The color of the ground was in him, the red earth,
    The smack and tang of elemental things.

.   .   .   .

    And when he fell in whirlwind, he went down
    As when a lordly cedar, green with boughs,

Goes down with a great shout upon the hills,
And leaves a lonesome place against the sky.

Lincoln, the Man of the People

4. He drew a circle that shut me out—
Heretic, rebel, a thing to flout.
But Love and I had the wit to win:
We drew a circle that took him in.

Outwitted

HENRY VAN DYKE (1852–1933)

A Renaissance man in an age of specialists, Van Dyke's multiple achievements recalled those of our pioneer statesmen and men of letters. As a Presbyterian clergyman, he reached the heights of his profession when chosen as pastor of the Brick Presbyterian Church in New York, yet he resigned in 1899 to become professor of English literature at Princeton for twenty-five years. On leaves of absence from his academic post he served as U.S. Minister to the Netherlands in the earlier years 1913–1916, and (even when he reached retirement age) as a Navy chaplain during World War I.

1. No man's credit is as good as his money.

2. Individuality is the salt of common life. You may have to live in a crowd, but you do not have to like it, nor subsist on its food.

3. It is with rivers as it is with people: the greatest are not always the most agreeable nor the best to live with.

4. Oh, London is a man's town; there's power in the air;
And Paris is a woman's town, with flowers in her hair.

America for Me

5. Not to the swift, the race:
Not to the strong, the fight;
Not to the righteous, perfect grace:
Not to the wise, the light.

Reliance

6. Self is the only prison that can ever bind the soul.

The Prison and the Angel

7.   Time is
Too slow for those who Wait,
Too swift for those who Fear,
Too long for those who Grieve,
Too short for those who Rejoice,
    But for those who Love
    Time is not.

On a sun dial, Saratoga Springs, New York

8. I shall grow old, but never lose life's zest,
Because the road's last turn will be the best.

The Zest of Life

THOMAS RILEY MARSHALL
(1854–1925)

THE power of fame bestowed by the "wise crack" in high places gave to Marshall, an otherwise undistinguished Vice President under President Wilson, a certain immortality. When he was discussing the question of inflation, while presiding over the Senate, he remarked:

What this country needs is a good five-cent cigar.

WILLIAM DUNCAN VANDIVER
(1854–1932)

FOR many years, and even today, there was no more eloquent expression of skepticism than, "I'm from Missouri." The phrase gained currency from a speech delivered by Vandiver in 1899 when, as a member of the House of Representatives, he spoke at a naval banquet in Philadelphia.

I come from a state that raises corn and cotton and cockleburs and Democrats, and frothy eloquence neither convinces nor satisfies me. I'm from Missouri; you've got to show me.

WILLIAM COWPER BRANN (1855–1898)

THIS commentator on the American scene of his day stands out as one of the newer breed of plain-spoken critics, not seeking immortality by his work, but salting the air with criticism. A Texan, he published a monthly magazine and a newspaper, both with the name of *The Iconoclast,* until he was shot by an outraged reader.

1. Boston runs to brains as well as to beans and brown bread. But she is cursed with an army of cranks whom nothing short of a straight-jacket or a swamp-elm club will ever control.

2. No man can be a patriot on an empty stomach.

3. It has the subtle flavor of an old pair of sox.

4. The Lydian notes of Andrew Carnegie as he warbles a riant roundelay in praise of poverty, or laments in pathetic spondees the woes of the man with spondulix.

5. We are slowly emerging from the crash of '93, and the cuckoos are cock-sure that a country fairly bursting with wealth was saved from the demnition bowwows by the blessed expedient of going into debt. *Speech, 1895*

EUGENE V. DEBS (1855–1926)

DEBS is remembered as a brilliant, controversial figure who has been called an irresponsible rabble-rouser and martyr for his principles. Successively laborer, labor leader, Socialist leader and [in World War I] imprisoned pacifist, this ex-president of the American Railway Union was the Socialist candidate for president five times. In 1920 while in prison he received 919,000 votes for the Presidency.

1. Wealth,—the savings of many in the hands of one.

2. I realize that there are certain limitations placed upon the

right of free speech. I may not be able to say all I think, but I am not going to say anything I do not think.

WALTER HINES PAGE (1855–1918)

SCHOLARLY journalist, author and eventually Ambassador under President Wilson to the Court of St. James, Page was a man of strong convictions. In his early years he crusaded for: reforms in agriculture, education and industry in his native South; later, before America's entrance in World War I, he advocated public support of Britain.

There is one thing better than good government, and that is government in which all the people have a part.

ELLA WHEELER WILCOX (1855–1919)

WITHOUT ever holding public office or crusading for anything in particular, this woman from Janesville, Wisconsin, became a national figure. She contributed stories to magazines, and the Hearst newspapers—but it was her poetry, still popular and much anthologized, which established her claim on our memories.

1. The world has a thousand creeds, and never a one have I;
   Nor a church of my own, though a thousand spires are
       pointing the way on high.
   But I float on the bosom of faith, that bears me along like
       a river;
   And the lamp of my soul is alight with love for life,
       and the world, and the Giver.

   Heresy

2. Talk happiness. The world is sad enough
   Without your woe. No path is wholly rough.

   .   .   .   .

Talk faith. The world is better off without
Your uttered ignorance and morbid doubt.

.   .   .   .

Talk health. The dreary, never-ending tale
Of mortal maladies is more than stale;
You cannot charm or interest or please
By harping on that minor chord, disease.
Say you are well, or all is well with you,
And God shall hear your words, and make them true.

Speech

3. Since life is short, we need to make it broad;
Since life is brief, we need to make it bright;
Then keep the old king's motto well in sight,
And let its meaning permeate each day
Whatever comes—"This, too, shall pass away."

This, Too, Shall Pass Away

4. It is easy to sit in the sunshine
    And talk to the man in the shade;
It is easy to float on a well-trimmed boat,
    And point out the places to wade.

Practice vs. Preaching

5. Laugh and the world laughs with you;
    Weep, and you weep alone;
For the sad old earth must borrow its mirth,
    But has trouble enough of its own.

.   .   .   .

Feast, and your halls are crowded;
    Fast, and the world goes by.

Solitude

6. We flatter those we scarcely know,
    We please the fleeting guest,
And deal full many a thoughtless blow
    To those who love us best.

Life's Scars

7. *I Will Be Worthy of It*

Title of poem

FRANCIS BELLAMY (1856–1931)

AS director of youth activities of the *Youth's Companion,* Bellamy first gave the "Pledge to the Flag" national prominence on the 400th anniversary of Columbus' discovery of America. Although its pledge is generally attributed to Upham, an owning partner of the *Youth's Companion,* Bellamy and the staff of *Youth's Companion* put it into its original form.

The first version given below is Upham's or Bellamy's in final form; the second, with additions in italics, was adopted by a joint resolution of Congress and signed by President Eisenhower in June, 1954.

1. I pledge allegiance to the flag of the United States and to the Republic for which it stands, one Nation, indivisible, with liberty and justice for all. (1892)

2. I pledge allegiance to the flag *of the United States of America* and to the Republic for which it stands, one Nation, *under God,* indivisible, with liberty and justice for all.

LOUIS DEMBITZ BRANDEIS (1856–1941)

THIS Boston-born, close friend of Oliver Wendell Holmes, Jr. and fellow liberal, was long his associate among the Justices of the United States Supreme Court. Brandeis's reputation for kindliness was matched only by his astuteness as a watchdog for individual rights.

1. Experience should teach us to be most on our guard to protect liberty when the government's purposes are beneficent.

Opinion: Olmstead vs. U.S., 1928

2. There must be a division not only of profits, but a division also of responsibilities . . . We must insist upon labor sharing the responsibilities for the result of the business. *Testimony, U.S. Commission on Industrial Relations, 1915*

KENYON COX (1856–1919)

WHO among us has not heard the admonition to "work for work's sake" if striving for true accomplishment? This is the proverb neatly coined into verse by Cox, who now ranks historically among America's leading portraitists, muralists and art critics.

> Work thou for pleasure—paint, or sing, or carve
> The thing thou lovest, though the body starves—
> Who works for glory misses oft the goal;
> Who works for money coins his very soul.
> Work thou for the work's sake, then, and it may be
> That these things shall be added unto thee.
>
> *Work*

WOODROW WILSON (1856–1924)

WILSON'S interests and accomplishments cover too vast a range for a thumbnail description to do them justice. Here was a President —a come-lately politician—who as historian, president of Princeton University and lecturer, would have been one of America's great men had he never been drawn into the world of politics.

1. I believe in democracy because it releases the energies of every human being.

2. It is just as hard to do your duty when men are sneering at you as when they are shooting at you.   *Speech, 1914*

3. There is such a thing as a man being too proud to fight. There is such a thing as a nation being so right that it does not need to convince others by force that it is right.   *Speech, May 10, 1915*

4. Politics I conceive to be nothing more than the science of the ordered progress of society along the line of greatest usefulness and convenience to itself.   *Speech, 1916*

5. One cool judgment is worth a dozen hasty councils. The thing to do is to supply light and not heat.   *Speech, 1916*

6. There must be, not a balance of power, but a community of power; not organized rivalries, but an organized common peace.
          Speech, 1917

7. A little group of wilful men representing no opinion but their own.   *His response to filibustering "isolationists"*

8. To such a task we dedicate our lives and our fortunes, everything that we are and everything that we have, with the pride of those who know that the day has come when America is privileged to spend her blood and her might for the principles that gave her birth and the peace which she has treasured. God helping her, she can do no other. . . . The world must be made safe for democracy.
Message to Congress asking for Declaration of War, April 2, 1917

9. I firmly believe in divine Providence. Without belief in Providence I think I should go crazy. Without God the earth would be a maze without a clue.

GERTRUDE F. (HORN) ATHERTON (1857–1948)

MRS. Atherton's career as an author, which was distinguished by its longevity and its variety, centered around San Francisco which she saw grow from a frontier mining town to a cosmopolitan city. She published her first historical novel, *The Doomswoman* in her mid-'thirties and the partly autobiographical *My San Francisco* two years before her death at ninety-one. Her most quoted work, however, was the novel *The Conqueror*, based on the life of Alexander Hamilton. Here are some of the views expressed there.

The perfect friendship of two men is the deepest and highest sentiment of which the finite mind is capable; women miss the best in life.

No matter how hard a man may labor, some woman is always in the background of his mind. She is the one reward of virtue.

CLARENCE SEWARD DARROW
(1857–1938)

THIS brilliant attorney, viciously tenacious in argument, won noted professional and financial success as a criminal lawyer. Later in life he left a lucrative practice to defend "causes." As legal counsel opposing William Jennings Bryan in the famous Scopes "evolution case" in Tennessee he won a unique place in the history of justice.

1. I don't believe in God because I don't believe in Mother Goose.

2. There is no such thing as justice—in or out of court.

3. The first half of our lives is ruined by our parents and the second half by our children.

4. At twenty a man is full of fight and hope. He wants to reform the world; when a man is seventy he still wants to reform the world but he knows he can't.

THORSTEIN VEBLEN
(1857–1929)

WHEN we speak of "conspicuous consumption" we're using one of many picturesque economic phrases coined by an introspective farm boy from Wisconsin with an insatiable desire for study. Veblen worked through Carleton College, Johns Hopkins, Yale and Cornell, later taught at Chicago, Stanford and Missouri Universities. Never very popular in his lifetime, his books nonetheless have become the basis of the school of thought sometimes described as institutional economics. Though he wrote in a highly artificial style, his satire won him lay readers. The following selections are from *The Theory of the Leisure Class,* 1899, Veblen's magnum opus.

With the exception of the instinct of self-preservation, the propensity for emulation is probably the strongest and most alert and persistent of the economics motives proper.

•   •   •   •

The dog commends himself to our favour by affording play to our propensity for mastery, and as he also is an item of expense, and commonly serves no industrial purpose, he holds a well-assured place in men's regard as a thing of good repute.

· · · ·

The visible imperfections of the hand-wrought goods, being honorific, are accounted marks of superiority in point of beauty, or serviceability, or both. Hence has arisen that exaltation of the defective, of which John Ruskin and William Morris were such eager spokesmen in their time.

· · · ·

. . . the womanliness of woman's apparel resolves itself . . . into the more effective hindrance to useful exertion offered by the garments peculiar to women.

· · · ·

Priestly vestments show, in accentuated form, all the features that have been shown to be evidence of a servile status and a vicarious life.

· · · ·

The walking-stick serves the purpose of an advertisement that the bearer's hands are employed otherwise than in useful effort, and it therefore has utility as an evidence of leisure.

· · · ·

To meet the requirements of the highest economic efficiency under modern conditions, the world process must habitually be apprehended in terms of quantitative, dispassionate force and sequence.

· · · ·

The adoption of the cap and gown is one of the striking atavistic features of modern college life.

· · · ·

The classics have scarcely lost in absolute value as a voucher of scholastic respectability, since for this purpose it is only necessary that the scholar should be able to put in evidence some learning which is conventionally recognized as evidence of wasted time.

· · · ·

As felicitous an instance of futile classicism as can well be found is the conventional spelling of the English language. English orthography satisfies all the requirements of the canons of reputability under the law of conspicuous waste. It is archaic, cumbrous, and ineffective; its acquisition consumes much time and effort; failure to acquire it is easy of detection.

SAM WALTER FOSS (1858–1911)

THIS New England journalist gradually emerged as poet voicing a "new" America of simple values and simple virtues.

1. Bring me men to match my mountains,
   Bring me men to match my plains,
   Men with empires in their purpose
   And new eras in their brains.

   The Coming American

2. The woods were made for the hunter of dreams,
   The brooks for the fishers of song;
   To the hunters who hunt for the gunless game
   The streams and the woods belong.

   The Bloodless Sportsmen

3. Let me live in my house by the side of the road
      Where the race of men go by;
   They are good, they are bad, they are weak, they are
         strong,
      Wise, foolish—so am I.
   Then why should I sit in the scorner's seat,
      Or hurl the cynic's ban?
   Let me live in my house by the side of the road
      And be a friend of man.

   The House by the Side of the Road

4. He had a startling genius, but somehow it didn't emerge;
      Always on the evolution of things that wouldn't
         evolve;

> Always verging toward some climax, but he never reached
> the verge;
> Always nearing the solution of some theme he could
> not solve.
>   *The Inventor*

THEODORE ROOSEVELT (1858–1919)

THE twenty-sixth President was in many ways the prototype of the "modern American." Born into an established and economically independent family in New York, and a graduate of Harvard, he broke away from the social and political traditions of his class. In the White House he saw nothing strange about drinking his dinner wine from his personal jeweled goblet and then going into a conference to fight for better conditions for the laboring man. Lively interest in his life continues to the present day. A new biography by Noel F. Busch, published in 1963, has had a great success.

1. Far better it is to dare mighty things, to win glorious triumphs, even though checkered by failure, than to take rank with those poor spirits who neither enjoy much nor suffer much, because they live in the gray twilight that knows not victory nor defeat.   *Speech, 1899*

2. I am as strong as a bull moose and you can use me to the limit.   *Letter, 1900*

3. There is a homely adage which runs, "Speak softly and carry a big stick; you will go far."   *Speech, 1901*

4. We demand that big business give the people a square deal; in return we must insist that when anyone engaged in big business honestly endeavors to do right he shall himself be given a square deal.

5. I took the Canal Zone and let Congress debate, and while the debate goes on the canal does also.

6. The men with the muck-rake are often indispensable to the well-being of society; but only if they know when to stop raking the muck.   *Speech, 1906*

7. It is difficult to make our material condition better by the best laws, but it is easy enough to ruin it by bad laws.

8. I wish to preach, not the doctrine of ignoble ease, but the doctrine of the strenuous life.

9. It is well indeed for our land that we of this generation have learned to think nationally.

10. Nine-tenths of wisdom consists in being wise in time.

11. My hat is in the ring.   *Speech, 1912*

KATHERINE LEE BATES (1859–1929)

ON Independence Day, 1895, the magazine the *Congregationalist* published a new hymn that ranks very close to the "Star Spangled Banner" and "America" in prestige and popularity. Miss Bates' work was hardly an accident for she was a highly successful poet. This was her jewel—honored even by Wellesley, her college, which years later commissioned murals to illustrate it.

> O beautiful for patriot dreams
>> That sees beyond the years
> Thine alabaster cities gleam
>> Undimmed by human tears!
>>> America! America!
>> God shed his grace on thee,
> And crown thy good with brotherhood
>> From sea to shining sea!

America the Beautiful

JOHN DEWEY (1859–1952)

DEWEY'S life was long and active; he published his last book at the age of ninety. As philosopher and educator, he probably influenced more students than any other American, with the possible exception of Santayana. This foremost authority on progressive education started his teaching career in the 1880's, but spent his maturity at Columbia University from 1904 to 1930, when he "retired" as professor emeritus, and devoted all his time to writing.

Experience alone cannot deliver to us necessary truths; truths completely demonstrated by reason. Its conclusions are particular, not universal.

.　　.　　.　　.

Every great advance in science has issued from a new audacity of imagination. *The Quest for Certainty*

ELBERT HUBBARD (1859–1915)

HUBBARD, who died with his wife in the sinking of the "Lusitania," was an Indiana-born author. He was an active promoter of handicrafts and published a little magazine called the *Philistine,* which had an appeal to readers out of all proportion to its circulation. His most famous article was "A Message to Garcia," based on an incident that took place during the Spanish-American War. His earthy philosophical expressions are quoted often today.

1. It is not book learning young men need, nor instruction about this and that, but a stiffening of the vertebrae which will cause them to be loyal to a trust, to act promptly, concentrate their energies, do a thing—"carry a message to Garcia."

A Message to Garcia

2. The path of civilization is paved with tin cans.

3. The man who is anybody and who does anything is surely going to be criticized, vilified, and misunderstood. This is a part of the penalty for greatness, and every great man understands it; and understands, too, that it is no proof of greatness. The final proof of greatness lies in being able to endure contumely without resentment. *Get Out or Get in Line*

4. As a career, the business of an orthodox preacher is about as successful as that of a celluloid dog chasing an asbestos cat through Hell.

5. Make two grins grow where there was only a grouch before.

6. A man's acts are usually right, but his reasons seldom are.

CHARLES E. STANTON (1859–1933)

FOUR words from this quotation have been incorrectly attributed to General John J. Pershing. For the record, they were uttered by Colonel Stanton as military representative of our government, at the traditional wreath laying ceremonies on Lafayette's Tomb, in Paris, on our Independence Day, 1917, recently after we had joined the allies.

America has joined forces with the Allied Powers, and what we have of blood and treasure are yours. Therefore it is with loving pride we drape the colors in tribute of respect to this citizen of your great republic. And here and now in the presence of the illustrious dead we pledge our hearts and our honor in carrying this war to a successful issue. *Lafayette, we are here*.

JANE ADDAMS (1860–1935)

OF all the facets of Miss Addams' full career—as author and leader in the woman suffrage and peace movements—her monument is Hull House, one of the first settlement houses in America, which she established with Ellen Gates Starr in 1889. This pioneering work deeply influenced many other cities to follow Chicago's lead and won for Miss Addams (with Nicholas Butler) the 1931 Nobel Peace Prize.

Private beneficence is totally inadequate to deal with the vast numbers of the city's disinherited. . . .

The common stock of intellectual enjoyment should not be difficult of access because of the economic position of him who would approach it. *Twenty Years at Hull House*

JOHN COLLINS BOSSIDY
(1860–1928)

FEW "toasts" given at dinners have spread so far or lived so long as this one.

> And this is good old Boston,
>> The home of the bean and the cod,
> Where the Lowells talk to the Cabots,
>> And the Cabots talk only to God.
>> *At Holy Cross Alumni Dinner, 1910*

WILLIAM JENNINGS BRYAN
(1860–1925)

THE "Great Commoner," unsuccessful Presidential candidate, orator and editor may be termed one of the great spellbinders of all time. Aside from his success as a politician he was a "star" of the Chatauqua circuit. His popularity and fees as a lecturer supported an entourage in a private railroad car. Many remember his verbal onslaughts against the theory of evolution when he pitted his talents as an attorney for the state against Clarence Darrow in the Scopes trial.

1. You shall not press down upon the brow of labor this crown of thorns, you shall not crucify mankind upon a cross of gold.   *At the Democratic National Convention, 1896*

2. If the Father deigns to touch with divine power the cold and pulseless heart of the buried acorn and to make it burst forth from its prison walls, will He leave neglected in the earth the soul of man made in the image of his Creator?   *The Prince of Peace*

3. There is no more reason to believe that man descended from some inferior animal than there is to believe that a stately mansion has descended from a small cottage.

At the Scopes Trial, 1925

CHARLES FROHMAN (1860–1915)

MOVING early from his birthplace in Ohio to become a New York theater box-office clerk, by the time Frohman died in the sinking of the "Lusitania," he was probably the most famous of American impresarios. He introduced a generation of great stars including Maude Adams, John Drew and Ethel Barrymore.

Why fear death? It is the most beautiful adventure in life.

HAMLIN GARLAND (1860–1940)

GARLAND made his living primarily as a popular travel lecturer in the years before motion pictures and broadened public travel diminished this field of interest. He was a celebrated regionalist.

Do you fear the force of the wind,
    The slash of the rain?
Go face them and fight them,
    Be savage again.

. . . .

The palms of your hands will thicken,
    The skin of your cheek will tan,
You'll go ragged and weary and swarthy,
    But you'll walk like a man!

Do You Fear the Wind?

JAMES GIBBONS HUNEKER (1860–1921)

HUNEKER, a Philadelphia-born music critic, virtually dominated this field. He contributed to various New York newspapers from 1902 until his death. But his satiric wit shone forth best in his essays.

Many years ago I learned to discount the hurry and flurry of New York. We are no busier than Bridgeport or Jersey City, but we pretend we are. It is necessary for our municipal vanity to squeeze and jam and rush and crush.

BOISE PENROSE (1860–1921)

AS Pennsylvania political leader and senator, Penrose may be assumed to have known whereof he once spoke.

> Political office is the last refuge of the incompetent.
> > Are lighter than the blown thistle down;
> She bears the glamour of one star
> > Upon her violet crown.

Dusk

OWEN WISTER (1860–1938)

WHAT American boy of the last two generations has not, at least once, drawn his cap pistol from its holster and challenged playmates with this line from the novel *The Virginian*.

> When you call me that, *smile!*

JOE HILL (1861?–1910)

SOMETIMES known as the Hobo Poet, Hill has had many poems attributed to him, all full of sardonic humor.

> You will eat bye and bye
> > In that glorious land above the sky;

Work and pray, live on hay,
    You'll get pie in the sky when you die.
                        The Preacher and the Slave

JOHN KENDRICK BANGS
(1862–1922)

BORN in Yonkers, New York, and graduated from Columbia in 1883, Bangs was monumentally successful in the field of humorous literature. While serving in editorial posts on various magazines he published more than thirty books of humorous stories, verse and plays.

1. Be sure to keep a mirror always nigh
        In some convenient, handy sort of place,
    And now and then look squarely in thine eye,
        And with thyself keep ever face to face.
                                    Face to Face

2. I think mankind by thee would be less bored
    If only thou wert not thine own reward.
                            A Hint to Virtue

3. I have no dog, but it must be
    Somewhere there's one belongs to me—
    A little chap with wagging tail,
    And dark brown eyes that never quail.

                                        My Dog

4. I never seen a night
    So dark there wasn't light
    Somewheres about if I took care
    To strike a match and find out where.

                                A Philosopher

5. To dig and delve in nice clean dirt
    Can do a mortal little hurt.

                                    Gardening

6. The word for me is Joy, just simple Joy.

                                    The Word

ALBERT J. BEVERIDGE (1862–1927)

MANY think the term "grass roots" is old Americana; on the contrary it was coined in 1912, by Beveridge, a noted Indiana senator and historian, who used the expression in a speech before the Bull Moose Convention, 1912, at which Theodore Roosevelt was nominated as the new party's presidential candidate.

This party comes from the grass roots. It has grown from the soil of the people's hard necessities.

JAMES W. BLAKE (1862–1935)

AMERICA was becoming a country of poets and troubadors, many of whom contributed enduring songs to the native folios. This, music for which was written by Charles B. Lawlor, is one of them.

East Side, West Side, all around the town,
The tots sang "Ring-a-rosie," "London Bridge is
falling down";
Boys and girls together, me and Mamie O'Rourke
Tripped the light fantastic on the sidewalks of New
York.

The Sidewalks of New York

CARRIE JACOBS BOND (1862–1946)

THIS woman with as much determination as talent, born in Janesville, Wisconsin turned to undeveloped musical talents when widowhood left her desperate. Eventually she earned both fame and fortune as lyricist and composer, performed her own compositions, even published some of them. Her favorite is this one.

Well, this is the end of a perfect day,
Near the end of a journey, too;
But it leaves a thought that is big and strong,
With a wish that is kind and true.
For mem'ry has painted this perfect day
With colors that never fade,
And we find at the end of a perfect day,
The soul of a friend we've made.

A Perfect Day

NICHOLAS MURRAY BUTLER (1862–1947)

FOR forty-three years, Butler was president of Columbia University, which he helped expand from Columbia College. His appointment to this post continued an already distinguished career as educator, politician Nobel Prize winner and active worker for peace.

An expert is one who knows more and more about less and less.

JOHN JAY CHAPMAN (1862–1933)

NEW York-born and Harvard-educated, Chapman decided after ten years of law practice that he was more suited to writing, and thereafter made it his career, as friend and biographer of the Boston circle.

1. The New Testament, and to a very large extent the Old is the soul of man. You cannot criticize it. It criticizes you.
2. New York is not a civilization; it is a railroad station.

WILLIAM SYDNEY PORTER (O. HENRY) (1862–1910)

BORN in North Carolina, Porter wandered to Texas where his career as a bank teller and newspaperman stopped abruptly when a shortage of bank funds was charged to him. Sentenced for three years, he developed his style of writing short, colorful stories with a twist and emerged from prison to a short but brilliant career.

1. In dress, habits, manners, provincialism, routine and narrowness, he acquired that charming insolence, that irritating completeness, that sophisticated crassness, that overbalanced poise that makes the Manhattan gentlemen so delightfully small in his greatness.

Defeat of the City

2. If there ever was an aviary over-stocked with jays it is that Yaptown-on-the-Hudson called New York. *The Gentle Grafter*

3. He was outwardly decent and managed to preserve his aquarium, but inside he was impromptu and full of unexpectedness. *The Octapus Marooned*

4. East is East, and West is San Francisco, according to Californians. Californians are a race of people; they are not merely inhabitants of a State. *A Municipal Report*

5. If men knew how women pass the time when they are alone, they'd never marry. *Memoirs of a Yellow Dog*

6. She would have made a splendid wife, for crying only made her eyes more bright. *No Story*

7. A man asleep is certainly a sight to make angels weep. Now, a woman asleep you regard as different. No matter how she looks, you know it's better for all hands for her to be that way.

The Hiding of Black Bill

CHARLES EVANS HUGHES (1862–1948)

THIS gentle, bearded man—who, in a close election lost the presidency to Wilson—still maintained after half a century of public service as Secretary of State, Chief Justice of the United States and numerous other "greats" in office, the calm, reflective manner of the classroom where he might have remained as a law professor.

1. We are under a Constitution, but the Constitution is what the judges say it is. *Speech, 1907*

2. While democracy must have its organization and controls, its vital breath is individual liberty.   *Speech, 1939*

WALT MASON (1862–1939)

WHILE more and more serious matters complicated the American scene, whimsical rhymsters and commentators like Mason kept a humorous perspective by their homely comments.

1. The statesman throws his shoulders back and straightens
      out his tie,
   And says, "My friends, unless it rains, the weather will
      be dry."
   And when this thought into our brains has percolated
      through,
   We common people nod our heads and loudly cry, "How
      true!"

The Statesman

2. Little drops of water poured into the milk, give the milk-man's daughter lovely gowns of silk. Little grains of sugar mingled with the sand, make the grocer's assets swell to beat the band.

Little Things

EDITH (JONES) WHARTON (1862–1937)

THIS author of more than fifty volumes of short stories and novels, including the celebrated *The Age of Innocence* and *Ethan Frome*, was one of the first gifted members of New York's "society" of her day to look ironically at its mores—perhaps with excessive snobbery. At the age of forty-five she made France her permanent home.

1. I was never allowed to read the popular American children's books of my day because, as my mother said, the children spoke bad English *without the author's knowing it.*

.   .   .   .

Summer afternoon—summer afternoon; to me those have always been the two most beautiful words in the English language.

(Henry James to E.W.)

.   .   .   .

My parents and their group, though they held literature in great esteem, stood in nervous dread of those who produced it. Washington Irving, Fitz-Greene Halleck and William Dana were the only representatives of the disquieting art who were deemed uncontaminated by it; though Longfellow, they admitted, if a popular poet, was nevertheless a gentleman.   *A Backward Glance*

2. There are two ways of spreading light: to be the candle or the mirror that reflects it.   *Vesalius in Zante*

3. My little old dog:
   A heart-beat at my feet.   *A Lyrical Epigram*

OLIVER HERFORD (1863–1935)

THIS quotable adoptive American migrated from England to settle in this country where he wrote and illustrated his delightful books that have added so much to our store of humor.

1. Children, behold the Chimpanzee.
       He sits on the ancestral tree
   From which we sprang in ages gone.
       I'm glad we sprang; had we held on
   We might, for aught that I can say,
       Be horrid Chimpanzees today.

The Chimpanzee

2. It is not fair to visit all
   The blame on Eve, for Adam's fall;
   The most Eve did was to display
   Contributory neglige.

Eve: Apropos de Rien

3. O Mongoose, where were you that day
   When Mistress Eve was led astray?
   If you'd but seen the serpent first,
   Our parents would not have been cursed.

A Child's Natural History

GEORGE SANTAYANA (1863–1952)

THOUGH brought to the United States at the age of nine and educated at Harvard, this Spanish-born philosopher-poet remained a Spanish subject. Santayana taught in Harvard's philosophy department from 1889 until he retired in order to write in 1912. While in residence in an Italian convent he produced some of the most beautiful and thoughtful writing in modern English prose and poetry. To cap his career, Santayana wrote and published when he was seventy-two his only novel, *The Last Puritan,* which was a great popular success among readers who had never heard of his earlier intellectual triumphs.

1. The human race, in its intellectual life, is organized like the bees; the masculine soul is a worker, sexually atrophied, and essentially dedicated to impersonal and universal arts; the feminine is a queen, infinitely fertile, omnipresent in its brooding industry, but passive and abounding in intuitions without method and passions without justice.   *The Life of Reason*

2. England is the paradise of individuality, eccentricity, heresy, anomalies, hobbies, and humours.

.   .   .   .

The world is a perpetual caricature of itself; at every moment it is the mockery and the contradiction of what it is pretending to be.

.   .   .   .

There is no cure for birth and death save to enjoy the interval.

.   .   .   .

I like to walk about amidst the beautiful things that adorn the world; but private wealth I should decline, or any sort of personal possessions, because they would take away my liberty.

.   .   .   .

My atheism, like that of Spinoza, is true piety towards the universe and denies only gods fashioned by men in their own image, to be servants of their human interests.

Soliloquies in England

3. There is nothing impossible in the existence of the super-natural. Its existence seems to me decidedly probable.

The Genteel Tradition at Bay

4. Civilization is perhaps approaching one of those long winters that overtake it from time to time. Romantic Christendom —picturesque, passionate, unhappy episode—may be coming to an end. Such a catastrophe would be no reason for despair.

American life is a powerful solvent. It seems to neutralise every intellectual element, however tough and alien it may be, and to fuse it in the native good-will, complacency, thoughtlessness, and optimism.

All his life he [the American] jumps into the train after it has started and jumps out before it has stopped; and he never once gets left behind, or breaks a leg.

Character and Opinion in the United States

5. It is a great advantage for a system of philosophy to be substantially true. *The Unknowable*

6. The young man who has not wept is a savage, and the old man who will not laugh is a fool. *Dialogues in Limbo*

7. Beauty is pleasure regarded as the quality of a thing.

. . . .

The infinity which moves us is the sense of multiplicity in uniformity. Accordingly, things which have enough multiplicity, as the lights of a city seen across water, have an effect similar to that of the stars, if less intense; whereas a star, if alone, because the multiplicity is lacking, makes a wholly different impression.

. . . .

Beauty as we feel it is something indescribable; what it is or what it means can never be said.

. . . .

Beauty is a pledge of the possible conformity between the soul and nature, and consequently a ground of faith in the suprem-acy of good. *The Sense of Beauty*

8. That life is worth living is the most necessary of assump-tions, and, were it not assumed, the most impossible of conclusions.

The Life of Reason

ERNEST LAWRENCE THAYER (1863–1940)

IN 1888 the *San Francisco Examiner* printed a long poem, appropriately timed for the baseball season, about the woes of a mythical baseball player who struck out. The fame of "Casey at the Bat" soon spread and the name of its author with it.

There was ease in Casey's manner as he stepped into his
  place,
There was pride in Casey's bearing, and a smile on Casey's
  face,
And when, responding to the cheers, he lightly doffed his
  hat,
No stranger in the crowd could doubt 'twas Casey at the
  bat.

.   .   .   .   .

From the benches black with people there went up a
  muffled roar,
Like the beating of the storm-waves on a stern and distant
  shore.

.   .   .   .   .

With a smile of Christian charity great Casey's visage
  shone;
He stilled the rising tumult; he bade the game go on.

.   .   .   .   .

Oh! somewhere in this favored land the sun is shining
  bright;
The band is playing somewhere, and somewhere hearts
  are light,
And somewhere men are laughing and somewhere children
  shout,
But there is no joy in Mudville, mighty Casey has struck
  out.

Casey at the Bat

ARTHUR BRISBANE (1864–1936)

THE irony, or honesty, of egotism was most aptly expressed by Brisbane, long a leading newspaper editor and columnist, in his definition of editorial success—a definition he evidently applied to himself.

Writing good editorials is chiefly telling people what they think, not what you think.

RICHARD HOVEY (1864–1900)

"A Stein Song" was the most enduring among several promising works of Hovey, whose untimely death interrupted what might have been a great career. Born in Illinois and a graduate of Dartmouth, he also translated the poems of Maeterlinck.

1. Comrades, pour the wine tonight
   For the parting is with dawn!
   Oh, the clink of cups together,
   With the daylight coming on!

   Comrades

2. I am fervent with the sunset,
        I am fateful with the bay,
   For the wander-thirst is on me
        And my soul is in Cathay.

   A Sea Gypsy

3. For it's always fair weather
   When good fellows get together
   With a stein on the table and a good song ringing clear.

   A Stein Song

4. I do not know beneath what sky
        Nor on what seas shall be thy fate;
   I only know it shall be high,
        I only know it shall be great.

   Unmanifest Destiny

5. There are worser ills to face
      Than foemen in the fray;
   And many a man has fought because—
      He feared to run away.

                          The Marriage of Guenevere

WILLIAM LYON PHELPS
(1865–1943)

MOST indicative of the character of "Billy" Phelps was the fact that in 1931, after nearly forty consecutive years of teaching English literature at Yale (his alma mater) he could write a book entitled, *The Excitement of Teaching*. Lovable, human, he was nevertheless an astute critic with his share of opinions. The public's first acquaintance with his serio-whimsical mind came in 1933 when, on the occasion of his retirement, he made a broadcast on the subject of books.

1. You can learn more about human nature by reading the Bible than by living in New York.

2. The habit of reading is one of the greatest resources of mankind; and we enjoy reading books that belong to us much more than if they are borrowed. A borrowed book is like a guest in the house; it must be treated with punctiliousness, with a certain considerate formality. You must see that it contains no damage . . . and then, some day, although this is seldom done, you really ought to return it.

.   .   .   .

But your own books belong to you; you treat them with that affectionate intimacy that annihilates formality. Books are for use, not for show; you should own no book that you are afraid to mark up, or afraid to place on the table, wide open and face down. A good reason for marking favorite passages in books is that this practice enables you to remember more easily the significant sayings, to refer to them quickly, and then in later years, it is like visiting a forest where you once blazed a trail.

WILLIAM EDGAR BORAH
(1865–1940)

FOR thirty-three years Senator from one of the least populous states, Idaho, Borah became a national figure by opposing with equal force and outstanding oratory the conservatives of his own Republican Party, the League of Nations proposal by Woodrow Wilson, and most of F. D. Roosevelt's New Deal measures. Noted as an interpreter of the Constitution he was sometimes called the "Great Opposer."

Peace upon any other basis than national independence . . . is fit only for slaves. *League of Nations Senate Debate, 1919*

LOGAN PEARSALL SMITH
(1865–1946)

BORN in New Jersey, Smith went at the age of twenty-three to England where he thereafter lived and wrote. However, he took with him a heritage from the New World that gave his essays and books a claim as Americana. This heritage is best seen in "Afterthoughts."

There are two things to aim at in life; first, to get what you want; and, after than, to enjoy it. Only the wisest of mankind achieve the second.

Happiness is a wine of the rarest vintage, and seems insipid to a vulgar taste.

How awful to reflect that what people say of us is true!

Solvency is entirely a matter of temperament and not of income.

That we should practise what we preach is generally admitted; but anyone who preaches what he and his hearers practise must incur the gravest moral disapprobation.

It is almost always worthwhile to be cheated; people's little frauds have an interest which more than repays what they cost us.

Why are happy people not afraid of Death, while the insatiable and the unhappy so abhor that grim feature?

The indefatigable pursuit of an unattainable Perfection, even though it consists in nothing more than in the pounding of an old piano, is what alone gives a meaning to our life on this unavailing star.

A best-seller is the gilded tomb of a mediocre talent.

What I like in an author is not what he says, but what he whispers.

Afterthoughts

GEORGE ADE (1866–1944)

HAD the gifted Ade, native of Indiana and graduate of Purdue, written only the satirically humorous newspaper sketches, he would have been famous enough for one life; but his equally successful plays, comedy librettos and film scenarios, reveal another side of his talent and America's greatness: a man could live and work exclusively in the Middle West and speak graphically the voice of this growing country.

1. Only the more rugged mortals should attempt to keep up with current literature.

The Time to enjoy a European trip is about Three Weeks after Unpacking.

A good folly is worth what you pay for it.

In uplifting, get underneath.

To insure Peace of Mind ignore the Rules and Regulations.

Stay with the Procession or you will Never Catch up.

Draw your Salary before Spending it.

For Parlor Use the Vague Generality is a Life-Saver.

Fables in Slang

2. Last night at twelve I felt immense,
But now I feel that thirty cents.

.   .   .   .

But, R-e-m-o-r-s-e!
The water-wagon is for me;

It is no time for mirth and laughter,
The cold, gray dawn of the morning after!

The Sultan of Sulu

GELETT BURGESS (1866–1951)

IT may be difficult to remember any of the other works of the prolific Boston-born artist and humorist, who ironically chose engineering as his field at Massachusetts Institute of Technology, but his "The Purple Cow" seems imperishable.

I never saw a Purple Cow,
    I never hope to see one;
But I can tell you, anyhow,
    I'd rather see than be one!

The Purple Cow

BERT LESTON TAYLOR (B.L.T.) (1866–1921)

FOR the last twelve years of his life, Taylor's name, contracted to his initials, headed probably the most sophisticated newspaper column in America—"A Line o' Type or Two," in the Chicago *Tribune*. Editorial, humorous, occasionally poetic, it set the pattern for a new type of journalism, soon to be copied by many others.

1. When quacks with pills political would dope us,
    When politics absorb the livelong day,
I like to think about the star Canopus.
    So far, so far away!

Canopus

2. Hate of the millions who've choked you down,
In country kitchen or house in town,
We love a thousand, we hate but one,

With a hate more hot than the hate of the Gun—
    Bread Pudding!

                         Chant of Hate for Bread Pudding

3. Everywhere I look I see—
    Fact or fiction, life or play,
Still the little game of Three:
    B and C in love with A.

                                    Old Stuff

4. When my sun of life is low,
    When the dewy shadows creep,
Say for me before I go,
    "Now I lay me down to sleep."

                                  Sundown

FINLEY PETER DUNNE (1867–1936)

IN 1893, several years before B.L.T. started his *Tribune* column, Dunne began writing, in the Chicago *Evening Post* a series of sketches, signed "Mr. Dooley," which in Irish-American dialect, commented on the American scene. Mr. Dooley was so real to his readers that Dunne's own identity was submerged in that of his creation.

1. Th' dead ar-re always pop'lar. I knowed a society wanst to vote a monyment to a man an' refuse to help his fam'ly, all in wan night.   *On Charity*

2. Life'd not be worth livin' if we didn't keep our inimies.

                     On New Year's Resolutions

3. No matter whether th' constitution follows th' flag or not, th' Supreme Court follows th' iliction returns.

                     The Supreme Court's Decision

4. I think a lie with a purpose is wan iv th' worst kind an' th' mos' profitable.   *On Lying*

5. What's fame, afther all, me la-ad? 'Tis apt to be what some wan writes on ye'er tombstone.   *Fame*

WILLIAM TYLER PAGE (1868–1942)

ON a day in the spring of 1917, when the United States was heading inevitably toward war with Germany, Page, then Clerk of the House of Representatives, sat down and wrote the only formal prose he is known ever to have penned. When he showed it to the political leaders, it was adopted on April 3, 1918 by resolution of the House of Representatives, as "The American's Creed."

I believe in the United States of America as a Government of of the people, by the people, for the people; whose just powers are derived from the consent of the governed; a democracy in a republic, a sovereign Nation of many sovereign States; a perfect Union one and inseparable; established upon those principles of freedom, equality, justice and humanity for which American patriots sacrificed their lives and fortunes. I therefore believe it is my duty to my country to love it, to support its Constitution, to obey its laws, to respect its flag, and to defend it against all enemies.

WILLIAM ALLEN WHITE (1868–1944)

IN contrast to Brisbane, whose career was cosmopolitan, White stayed in the little city of Emporia, Kansas, where he owned and edited the *Gazette*. But the "Kansas Sage" built an international reputation. Kindly, honest, and not afraid of the devil himself, he bespoke American aspirations and ideals to a world-wide audience.

1. This is a middle-class country, and the middle class will have its will and say. For the middle class is the real owner of American industry.

2. Liberty is the only thing you cannot have unless you are willing to give it to others.

EDGAR LEE MASTERS (1869–1950)

THE literary fame this lawyer won with his *Spoon River Anthology* in 1915 was accompanied by violent controversy over the realism of some of the characters he treated anonymously in his sharp characterizations of small-town American life.

O maternal earth which rocks the fallen leaf to sleep.

·   ·   ·   ·

The dust's for crawling, heaven's for flying,
    Wherefore, O Soul, whose wings are grown,
      Soar upward to the sun!

Spoon River Anthology

EDWIN ARLINGTON ROBINSON (1869–1935)

BECAUSE Robinson is one of America's most-quoted poets, it seems surprising that he was almost fifty before he made his first impression as a major poet. He was to go on to win three Pulitzer Prizes. One can detect a somber undertone of spirit often associated with his native Maine in these selections.

1. The promise is yours but not the sight;
    You see not what upon you tread;
  You have the ages for your guide,
    But not the wisdom to be led.

Cassandra

2. Life is the game that must be played:
    This truth, at least, good friend's, we know;
  So live and laugh, nor be dismayed
    As one by one the phantoms go.

Ballade by the Fire

3. Two kinds of gratitude: the sudden kind
   We feel for what we take; the larger kind
   We feel for what we give.

Captain Craig

4. Who of us, being what he is,
   May scoff at others' ecstacies?
   However we may shine today,
   More-shining ones are on the way.

Atherton's Gambit

(NEWTON) BOOTH TARKINGTON (1869–1946)

TO categorize this prolific Indiana writer is impossible. Despite a sophisticated education including terms at Phillips Exeter Academy and Purdue and Princeton Universities, Tarkington leaned naturally toward homely simplicity. His talent flowered in stories of the Middle West, novels of youth and historical themes. Throughout his work he scattered little morsels of his own philosophy.

Penrod was doing something very unusual and rare, something almost never accomplished except by colored people or by a boy in school on a spring day: he was really doing nothing at all. He was merely a state of being.

. . . .

There are two things that will be believed of any man whatsoever, and one of them is that he has taken to drink.   *Penrod*

BERNARD MANNES BARUCH (1870–   )

THIS son of a South Carolina surgeon impoverished by the Civil War, graduated from the College of the City of New York when he was nineteen, went on to become a millionaire investor before he was thirty. Beginning with important government assignments in World War I, he has been an economic advisor to every President and an intimate friend of Sir Winston Churchill.

1. America has never forgotten—and will never forget—the nobler things that brought her into being and that light her path—the path that was entered upon only 150 years ago. . . . How young she is! It will be centuries before she will adopt the maturity of custom—the clothing of the grave—that some people believe she is already fitted for.   *Accepting the Churchman Award, 1944*

2. We are here to make a choice between the quick and the dead. That is our business. Behind the black portent of the new atomic age lies a hope which, seized upon with faith, can work our salvation. If we fail, then we have damned every man to be the slave of fear. Let us not deceive ourselves: we must elect world peace or world destruction.

Address to the United Nations Atomic
Energy Commission as U.S. Representative, 1946

THEODORE DREISER (1871–1945)

A great realistic novelist, despite an awkward style, Dreiser has often been considered a dour iconoclast. At times his expression was purely felicitous, and his prose verged on poetry.

Art is the stored honey of the human soul, gathered on wings of misery and travail.   *Life, Art and America*

CALVIN COOLIDGE (1872–1933)

A man of cultivated reticence who delighted in the nickname of "Silent Cal," the twenty-ninth President, nevertheless talked more [and quotably] about more subjects than his reputation leads us to believe.

1. There is no right to strike against the public safety by anybody, anywhere, any time.

Telegram to Samuel Gompers
on the Boston police strike, while he
was Governor of Massachusetts, 1919

2. It would be folly to argue that the people cannot make political mistakes. They can and do make grave mistakes. They know it, they pay the penalty, but compared with the mistakes which have been made by every kind of autocracy they are unimportant.

3. The business of America is business.

4. After order and liberty, economy is one of the highest essentials of a free government.

5. It is only when men begin to worship that they begin to grow.

6. The foundations of our society and of our government rest so much on the teachings of the Bible, that it would be difficult to support them, if faith in these teachings should cease to be practically universal in this country.

7. I do not choose to run.

Declining the Presidential nomination, 1928

PATRICK F. O'KEEFE (1872–1934)

ONE wonders what bonus, if any, was awarded to O'Keefe, for framing one of the great modern sales slogans of America for the Society of American Florists in 1917. He certainly deserved one.

Say It With Flowers.

CARL LOTUS BACKER (1873–1945)

PART philosopher and part economist, Backer wrote and talked less than Thorstein Veblen, but his realism about social matters helped to shape much of the modern perspective.

Economic distress will teach man, if anything can, that realities are less dangerous than fantasies, that fact-finding is more effective than fault-finding.

.   .   .   .

The significance of man is that he is that part of the universe that asks the question, What is the significance of man? He alone can stand apart imaginatively and, regarding himself and the universe in their eternal aspects, pronounce a judgment: The significance of man is that he is insignificant and is aware of it.

Progress and Power

ARTHUR CHAPMAN (1873–1935)

LONG after "the West" dominates the rest of the country in population and economic development (as it is rapidly seeming to do in the 1960's), there will linger the feeling that its scenery, its climate and its people are somewhat different. The poetry of Chapman will have done much to perpetuate this image.

1. Out where the handclasp's a little stronger,
   Out where the smile dwells a little longer,
       That's where the West begins.

.   .   .   .

   Out where the skies are a trifle bluer,
   Out where friendship's a little truer.

.   .   .   .

   Where there's more of singing and less of sighing,
   Where there's more of giving and less of buying,
   And a man makes friends without half trying.

Out Where the West Begins

2. Oh, the quickly faded glory,
   Of the cowboy's brief, brief story!
   How the old range beckons vainly
       in the sunshine and the rain.

The Cowpuncher's Elegy

WILLIAM GREEN (1873–1952)

THE grand old man of labor, Green ruled the American Federation of Labor for a generation, his reign bridging the beginnings of workers' movements under men like Eugene V. Debs and the more aggressive leaders like John L. Lewis. This was his philosophy.

The labor union is an elemental response to the human instinct for group action in dealing with group problems.

Speech, 1925

ALFRED E. SMITH (1873–1944)

THIS former Governor of New York, and unsuccessful candidate for the Presidency (he ran against Herbert Hoover in 1928), was a true product of "the sidewalks of New York," and a "graduate" of Tammany Hall. He was one of democracy's plainest-spoken champions.

1. The American people never carry an umbrella. They prefer to walk in eternal sunshine.   *Speech, 1931*
2. All the ills of democracy can be cured by more democracy.
Speech, 1933

HERBERT CLARK HOOVER (1874–   )

IN the year before the compilation of this work, Mr. Hoover wrote and published two books, one concerning letters received from and written to children and the other on fishing. Thus continues to grow the legend of the thirty-first Presi- dent, resoundingly defeated by Franklin D. Roosevelt in 1932 because popular opinion blamed his administration for the Depression. Hoover's career extended from the time when he was a young engineer who helped build Peking's legation-compound defenses in the Boxer Rebellion. He made a great fortune before he entered his first public service in World War I and, at his own expense, surveyed our government after World War II, and presented the Hoover Reports on the reorganization of government.

1. They [the Bill of Rights] are as clear as the Ten Commandments. Among others, the freedom of worship, freedom of speech and of the press, the right of peaceable assembly, equality before the law, just trial for crime, freedom from unreasonable search, and security from being deprived of life, liberty or property without due process of law, are the principles which distinguish our civilization. Herein are the invisible sentinels which guard the doors of every home from invasion of coercion, intimidation and fear. Herein is the expression of the spirit of men who would forever be free.

2. While I can make no claim for having invented the term "rugged individualism," I should be proud to have invented it. It has been used by American leaders for over a half-century in eulogy of those God-fearing men and women of honesty whose stamina and character and fearless assertion of rights led them to make their own way in life.   *The Challenge of Liberty*

3. I suggest that the United Nations be reorganized without the Communist nations in it.   *Speech, 1950*

4. In my opinion, we are in danger of developing a cult of the Common Man, which means a cult of mediocrity.

JOHN D. ROCKEFELLER, JR.
(1874–1960)

THIS son of the great amasser of wealth spent a long life dedicated to the task of developing means for disposing money for the public good. He seldom spoke or wrote publicly, but one sentence of his "Our Family Creed," stated his philosophy.

I believe that every right implies a responsibility; every opportunity, an obligation; every possession, a duty.

GERTRUDE STEIN (1874–1946)

IF Gertrude Stein had not been born, it is possible that no writer of fiction would have thought to invent such a literary character. Despite her eccentricities she was kindly of disposition and generous with her talent and influence toward her coterie, who included Hemingway and Dreiser. She spent the majority of her later years in France, writing and presiding over a lifetime literary salon.

   1. Rose is a rose is a rose is a rose.   *Sacred Emily*

   2. Pigeons in the grass alas.   *Four Saints in Three Acts*

   3. In the United States there is more space where nobody is than where anybody is. This is what makes America what it is.

The Geographical History of America

LAUGHTER AND SOBER THOUGHT

ROBERT FROST (1875–1963)

FEW poets whose verse has the life and fire to come readily to quoting tongue have won recognition as late, and afterward lived so long to enjoy their success as Frost. Some of us recall vividly the picture of the wind-blown old gentlemen standing in bitterly cold weather to read a tribute at the Inaugural of President Kennedy. This was the man who remained an almost unrecognized itinerant teacher and workman until the age of forty, but whose recognition came so rapidly thereafter that his poetry has been the subject of major critical works.

1. Something there is that doesn't love a wall.

   .   .   .   .

   Good fences make good neighbors.

   Mending Wall

2. I'd like to get away from earth awhile
   And then come back to it and begin over.
   May no fate willfully misunderstand me
   And half grant what I wish and snatch me away
   Not to return. Earth's the right place for love:
   I don't know where it's likely to go better.

   Birches

3. Nothing to look backward to with pride,
   And nothing to look forward to with hope.

   The Death of the Hired Man

4. I shall be telling this with a sigh
   Somewhere ages and ages hence:
   Two roads diverged in a wood, and I—
   I took the one less traveled by,
   And that has made all the difference.

   The Road Not Taken

5. Never ask of money spent
   Where the spender thinks it went.
   Nobody was ever meant
   To remember or invent

What he did with every cent.

The Hardship of Accounting

HAROLD MacDONALD ANDERSON (1876–1940)

THROUGHOUT all of literature, we find sprinkled poems, essays and whole books inspired by current deeds. Ranking with these, and in a high place, is a brief editorial in The New York *Sun,* May 21, 1927.

Alone?

Is he alone at whose right hand rides Courage, with Skill within the Cockpit and Faith upon the left? Does solitude surround the brave when Adventure leads the way and Ambition reads the dials? Is there no company with him for whom the air is cleft by Daring and the darkness is made light by Enterprise?

Alone?

With what other companions would that man fly to whom the choice is given?

Lindbergh Flies Alone

WILLA (SIBERT) CATHER (1876–1947)

VIRGINIA-BORN and educated in the Middle West, this novelist had the energy to embrace a career of teaching, editing of major women's magazines, and prolific writing of fiction—so successfully that her collected works fill thirteen volumes.

1. Oh, this is the joy of a rose.
     That it blows,
   And goes.

In Rose-Time

2. No one can build his security upon the nobleness of another person.

Alexander's Bridge

3. There are only two or three human stories, and they go on repeating themselves as fiercely as if they had never happened before.   *O Pioneers!*

4. We all like people who do things, even if we only see their faces on a cigar-box lid.   *The Song of the Lark*

5. The universal human yearning for something permanent, enduring, without shadow of change.

Death Comes for the Archbishop

RANDOM HUMORISTS

HERE is a rare grouping of men noted primarily as humorists, dedicated to satirizing the contemporary scene. Samplings of their wit are so complementary that they might be quoted almost interchangeably. Their common quality is evanescence.

IRVIN SHREWSBURY COBB (1876–1944)

There is this to be said for New York City: it is the one densely inhabited locality—with the possible exception of hell—that has absolutely not a trace of local pride.

WILSON MIZNER (1876–1933)

I respect faith but doubt is what gets you an education. . . . A good listener is not only popular everywhere but after a while he knows something.

FRANK WARD O'MALLEY (1875–1932)

Life is just one damned thing after another.

LOUIS KAUFMAN ANSPACHER (1878–1947)

Marriage is that relation between man and woman in which the independence is equal, the dependence mutual, and the obligation reciprocal.

HENRY SEIDEL CANBY (1878–1961)

THROUGHOUT a long career as teacher and editor, Dr. Canby (Yale) probably has influenced the modern reading tastes of America as much as any other man, first as editor of the *Saturday Review of Literature* and subsequently as chairman of the Board of Judges of the Book-of-the-Month Club, until his retirement in 1958.

1. Arrogance, pedantry, and dogmatism are the occupational diseases of those who spend their lives directing the intellects of the young.   *Alma Mater*

2. We can put our children on wheels to see the world, but we cannot give them the kind of home that any town provided in the nineties, not at any price.   *The Age of Confidence*

HARRY EMERSON FOSDICK (1878–   )

A preacher, widely known particularly for his radio broadcasts, which like his pulpit sermons emphasized the practical relationship between religion and everyday life. His active career—spanning the period from ordination as a Baptist minister in 1903 to retirement in 1946—is credited with having ushered in a new style of preaching.

Democracy is based upon the conviction that there are extraordinary possibilities in ordinary people.

DON (DONALD ROBERT) MARQUIS (1878–1937)

THE technique that B.L.T. introduced in the Chicago *Tribune*— the columnist commenting and versifying on all subjects—found its counterpart in New York in 1912 when Marquis moved from a newspaper job in Atlanta, Georgia, to start a column for The *Sun,* the *Sun Dial.* Among Marquis's other piquant contributions were the observations of archie, the prescient cockroach, and his friend, mehitabel, the cat—never spelled with capitals or properly punctuated because archie's weight (pre-electric typewriter, of course) was insufficient to press down the shift bar of a typewriter.

1. The saddest ones are those that wear
   The jester's motley garb.
   The Tavern of Despair

2. The world has just one tale to tell, and it is very old,
a little tale—a simple tale—a tale that's easy told:
"There was a youth in Babylon who greatly loved a maid!"
   News From Babylon

3. A man has jest naturally got to have something to cuss around and boss, so's to keep himself from finding out he don't amount to nothing.   *Danny's Own Story*

4. Dreadful things are just as apt to happen when stupid people control a situation as when definitely ill-natured people are in charge.

.   .   .   .

All religion, all life, all art, all expression come down to this: to the effort of the human soul to break through its barrier of loneliness, of intolerable loneliness, and make some contact with another seeking soul, or with what all souls seek, which is (by any name) God.   *Chapters for the Orthodox*

5. There will be no beans in the Almost Perfect State.
   The Almost Perfect State

6. Publishing a column of verse is like dropping a rose petal down the Grand Canyon and waiting for the echo.

.   .   .   .

Poetry is what Milton saw when he was blind.

· · · ·

If you make people think they're thinking, they'll love you.
If you really make them think they'll hate you.

· · · ·

An Idea isn't responsible for the people who believe in it.

The Sun Dial

7. procrastination is the
   art of keeping up with yesterday

certain maxims of archy

dance mehitabel dance
caper and shake a leg
what little blood is left
will fizz like wine in a keg.

mehitabel dances with boreas

i have noticed that when chickens quit quarrelling over
their food they often find that there is enough for all
of them i wonder if it might not be the same way with
the human race.

archy's life of mehitabel

it is a cheering thought to think that god is on the
side of the best digestion.

archy does his part

there is bound to be a certain amount of
trouble running any country
if you are president the trouble happens to you
but if you are a tyrant you can arrange things so
that most of the trouble happens to other people.

· · · ·

too many creatures
both insects and humans
estimate their own value
by the amount of minor irritation
they are able to cause
to greater personalities than themselves.

archy's newest deal

the females of all species are most
dangerous when they appear to retreat

archy and mehitabel

CARL SANDBURG
(1878–   )

STILL active at this writing, Sandburg is akin to Frost in background, close to the soil, gentleness of spirit and love for things American. First a poet and a minstrel, Sandburg probably surprised himself by becoming a foremost authority on Abraham Lincoln. For many years pursuing a dual career in journalism, this poet was forty-two years old when recognition finally came with his poem "Chicago," which won a prize in the magazine *Poetry*.

1. The fog comes on little cat feet.

Fog

2. O prairie mother, I am one of your boys.
   I have loved the prairie as a man with a heart shot full
   of pain over love.

Prairie

3. When Abraham Lincoln was shoveled into the tombs, he
   forgot the copperheads and the assassin . . . in the
   dust, in the cool tombs.   *Cool Tombs*

4. Lay me on an anvil, O God.
   Beat me and hammer me into a crowbar.
   Let me pry loose old walls.
   Let me live and loosen old foundations.

Prayers of Steel

5. Look out how you use proud words.
   When you let proud words go, it is not easy to call them
   back.
   They wear long boots, hard boots.

   .   .   .   .

   (Look out how you use proud words.)

Primer Lesson

6. Hog Butcher for the World,

Tool Maker, Stacker of Wheat,
Player with Railroads and the Nation's Freight Handler;
Stormy, husky, brawling,
City of the Big Shoulders.

Chicago

ETHEL BARRYMORE (1879–1959)

MISS Barrymore's great success as a dramatic star on the stage and in films in her riper years all but obscured old memories of her delightful portrayals of enchanting ingenues: such as the one in the forgotten play *Sunday*. After its opening in 1894 there were so many curtain calls, that Miss Barrymore, in an impromptu talk to the audience, coined a popular quotation.

That's all there is; there isn't any more.

(JAMES) BRANCH CABELL (1879–1958)

CABELL, as a native Virginian and graduate of William and Mary College, came close to reviving the Jeffersonian tradition of Virginia scholars, who were masters of several careers. Professor of English and Greek, this novelist was equally at ease in fiction and non-fiction, serious philosophy and ironic humor.

Marrying a woman because you happen to be in love with her is about as logical a proceeding as throwing the cat out of the window because the rhododendrons are in bloom.

ALBERT EINSTEIN (1879–1955)

THE accomplishments of Dr. Einstein, like those of other great men, are impossible to describe briefly. Formulator of the theory of relativity, author of a short note to Franklin D. Roosevelt in 1939 to urge the president to investigate the possibility of atomic energy for the country's defense, this scientist's contributions are so diversified that few are fully aware of the fields he made his own.

1. I never think of the future. It comes soon enough.

2. I cannot believe that God plays dice with the Cosmos.

3. An empty stomach is not a good political adviser.

4. Imagination is more important than knowledge.

5. Every kind of peaceful cooperation among men is primarily based on mutual trust and only secondarily on institutions such as courts of justice and police.

6. The most beautiful and most profound emotion we can experience is the sensation of the mystical. It is the sower of all true science. He to whom this emotion is a stranger, who can no longer wonder and stand rapt in awe, is as good as dead. To know that what is impenetrable to us really exists, manifesting itself as the highest wisdom and the most radiant beauty which our dull faculties can comprehend only in their most primitive form—this knowledge, this feeling is at the center of true religiousness.

WILL ROGERS (1879–1935)

ROGERS in retrospect may be described in as many ways as the proverbial blind children described the elephant. From the night he stepped on stage in the Ziegfeld Follies to twirl a rope and comment off-the-cuff on current happenings, in his Claremore, Oklahoma, dialect, he was to be noted as stage star, movie star, lecturer, after-dinner speaker, writer and sage. Finally, at fame's peak, he died in a crash against an Alaska mountain, on a flight.

1. All I know is just what I read in the papers.

2. I never met a man I didn't like.

3. There is nothing so stupid as an educated man, if you get him off the thing he was educated in.

4. The Republicans have their split right after election and Democrats have theirs just before an election.

5. There is a lot of difference in pioneering for gold and pioneering for spinach.

SIMEON STRUNSKY (1879–1948)

FOR many years New Yorkers found a special delight in an anonymous column on the editorial pages of the *Evening Post* and later the *Times,* entitled "Topics of the Times." The passing of the years saw publication of the columns under Strunsky's signature. Unlike his more famous colleagues this Russian-born essayist wrote only prose and never indulged in the first-person singular pronoun.

1. New York has more hermits than will be found in all the forests, mountains and deserts of the United States.

2. The more you think of it the more you will be persuaded that night is primarily the time of the innocent industries, and for the most part the primitive industries, employing simple, innocent, primitive men, slow-speaking truck farmers, husky red-faced slaughterers in the abattoirs, solid German bakers, and milkmen. The milkman alone is enough to redeem the night from its undeserved reputation. A cartload of pasteurized milk for nurslings at four o'clock in the morning represents more service to civilization than a cartful of bullion on its way from the sub-Treasury to the vaults of a national bank five hours later.

HELEN KELLER (1880–   )

MUCH has been made of the fact that Miss Keller, blind and deaf from the age of two, learned to speak eloquently and to "hear," "read" and "see" with her fingers, under the devoted teaching of Miss Anne Sullivan. More miraculous was Miss Keller's use of this knowledge, the high intellectual caliber of her inspiring writings.

Keep your face to the sunshine and you cannot see the shadow.

.   .   .   .

There is no king who has not had a slave among his ancestors, and no slave who has not had a king among his.

. . . .

Literature is my Utopia. Here I am not disfranchised. No barrier of the senses shuts me out from the sweet, gracious discourse of my book-friends. They talk to me without embarrassment or awkwardness.   *The Story of My Life*

JOHN L. LEWIS (1880–   )

THIS embattled, Welsh-born labor leader, who at one time wielded unparalleled power over the labor force of this nation, and as a result, almost as great political power, spoke with eloquence. In probably his most celebrated and controversial speech, he expressed his disillusionment with the promises of the "New Deal."

Labor, like Israel, has many sorrows. Its women weep for their fallen and they lament for the future of the children of the race.   *Speech, 1937*

DOUGLAS MacARTHUR (1880–   )

GENERAL of the Army, commander of the victorious forces in the Pacific in World War II, MacArthur was dismissed by Truman in 1951 after a conflict of policies and personalities that is now history. However, among the honors accorded to General MacArthur on his return was a rare invitation to address a joint session of the Congress, at which he delivered his "valedictory."

Only those Americans who are willing to die for their country are fit to live.

. . . .

Old soldiers never die; they just fade away.
                    Quote from an old song.

GEORGE CATLETT MARSHALL (1880–1958)

GENERAL of the Army Marshall, Chief of Staff in World War II, later became President Truman's Secretary of State. While in this post he promulgated the "Marshall Plan" of assistance for former allies —a notable milestone in American policy—in a speech at Harvard.

Our policy is directed not against any country or doctrine but against hunger, poverty, desperation and chaos.

HENRY LOUIS MENCKEN (1880–1956)

MENCKEN and Nathan, separately and together, exerted major influence on American thought, and particularly on the generation of writers who followed them. Throughout his career, Mencken wrote for Baltimore newspapers, and with Nathan founded first the magazine *Smart Set* and afterward *American Mercury,* to which he contributed much of his iconoclastic work. Nathan's other professional work was primarily in the field of dramatic criticism.

1. To the man with an ear for verbal delicacies . . . there is in writing the constant joy of sudden discovery, of happy accident.

.   .   .   .

Poverty is a soft pedal upon all branches of human activity, not excepting the spiritual.

.   .   .   .

Injustice is relatively easy to bear; what stings is justice.
Formalism is the hall-mark of the national culture.

.   .   .   .

Time is a great legalizer, even in the field of morals.

A Book of Prefaces

2. All successful newspapers are ceaselessly querulous and bellicose. They never defend anyone or anything if they can help it; if the job is forced upon them, they tackle it by denouncing someone or something else.

The great artists of the world are never Puritans, and seldom even ordinarily respectable.

Prejudices

3. All the more pretentious American authors try to write chastely and elegantly; the typical literary product of the country is still a refined essay in the *Atlantic Monthly,* perhaps gently jocose but never rough—by Emerson, so to speak, out of Charles Lamb.

The American Language

GEORGE JEAN NATHAN (1882–1958) with MENCKEN

The American Credo

That all one has to do to gather a large crowd in New York is to stand on the curb a few minutes and gaze intently at the sky.

That the postmasters in small towns read all the postcards.

That all theater box-office employees are very impolite and hate to sell a prospective patron a ticket.

That all newspaper reporters carry notebooks.

That, when shaving in a railway train, a man invariably cuts himself.

That the jokes in *Punch* are never funny.

That nicotine keeps the teeth in a sound condition.

That the wife of a rich man always looks back wistfully into the past and wishes she had married a poor man.

That the quality of the champagne may be judged by the amount of noise the cork makes when it is popped.

278 / *Nathan with Mencken*

278 / *Nathan with Mencken*

That all French women are very passionate, and will sacrifice everything for love.

That beer is very fattening.

That the cloth used in suits made in England is so good it never wears out.

That Philadelphia is a very sleepy town.

That if one swallows an ounce of olive oil before going to banquet, one will never get drunk.

That the worst actress in the company is always the manager's wife.

That milking a cow is an operation demanding a special talent that is possessed only by yokels, and that a person born in a large city can never hope to acquire it.

GRANTLAND RICE (1880–1954)

A nationally prominent sports columnist, Rice was particularly fond of lapsing into rhyme, as in this definition of sportsmanship.

> Keep coming back for all they've got, and take it with a
>   grin
> When disappointment trips you up or failure barks your
>   shin;
> Keep coming back, and if at last you lose the game of
>   right,
> Let those who whipped you know at least they, too, have
>   had a fight.
>
> *Alumnus Football*

FRANKLIN PIERCE ADAMS (F.P.A.) (1881–1960)

RANKING equally with B.L.T. and Don Marquis among the philosopher-columnists, stood F.P.A., long of The New York *World*.

1. Christmas is over and Business is Business.
2. Ruthlessly pricking our gonfalon bubble,
   Making a Giant hit into a double,
   Words that are weighty with nothing but trouble:
   "Tinker to Evers to Chance."

   Baseball's Sad Lexicon

3. Then here's to the City of Boston,
        The town of the cries and the groans,
   Where the Cabots can't see the Kabotchniks,
        And the Lowells won't speak to the Cohns.

   Boston *

4. The rich man has his motor car,
        His country and his town estate.
   He smokes a fifty-cent cigar
        And jeers at Fate.

             .   .   .   .

   Yet though my lamp burn low and dim,
        Though I must slave for livelihood—
   Think you that I would change with him?
        You bet I would!

   The Rich Man

5. Echo again the words of Paine,
        Clear as a mountain stream is clear,
   Sane as a prairie breeze is sane,
        Sound again on the listening ear.

             .   .   .   .

   "These are the times that try men's souls."

   Ballade of the American Crisis

6. If, my dear, you seek to slumber,
        Count of stars an endless number;
   If you still continue wakeful,
        Count the drops that make a lakeful;
   Then, if vigilance yet above you
        Hovers, count the times I love you;

* See under J. C. Bossidy, page 235.

> And if slumber still repel you,
>   Count the time I do not tell you.
>
> *Lullaby*

MARY ANTIN (1881–1949)

HERE is the voice of the American immigrant at the end of the nineteenth century. Miss Antin (born in Russia and brought to America in childhood) began her writing career while still at Columbia.

So at last I was going to America! Really, really going, at last! The boundaries burst. The arch of heaven soared! A million suns shone out for every star. The winds rushed in from outer space, roaring in my ears, "America! America!"

The Promised Land

EDGAR ALBERT GUEST (1881–1959)

MANY readers will remember the time when the mention of Guest's name in "literary" conversations could start a heated argument. Could a man be considered a poet who, year after year, wrote a daily verse? Poet or versifier, with his rhymed homilies, Guest cultivated one of the largest popular followings of his generation.

1. Somebody said that it couldn't be done,
       But he with a chuckle replied
   That "maybe it couldn't," but he would be one
       Who wouldn't say so till he'd tried.

                .   .   .

   He started to sing as he tackled the thing
       That couldn't be done, and he did it.

It Couldn't Be Done

2. It takes a heap o' living' in a house t' make it home,

A heap o' sun an' shadder, an' ye sometimes have t' roam
Afore ye really 'preciate the things ye lef' behind,
An' hunger fer 'em somehow, with 'em allus on yer mind.

Home

3. The things that haven't been done before,
    Those are the things to try;
Columbus dreamed of an unknown shore
    At the rim of the far-flung sky.

The Things That Haven't Been Done Before

4. I'd rather see a sermon than hear one any day;
I'd rather one should walk with me than merely tell the way.

Sermons We See

5. How do you tackle your job each day?
    Are you scared of the job you find?
Do you grapple the task that comes your way
    With a confident, easy mind?

How Do You Tackle Your Work?

WILLIAM McFEE (1881–   )

THE English-born McFee built his literary reputation on sea stories, of which *Casuals of the Sea* (1916) was his most widely recognized work. He settled in the United States in 1911, after spending some years on the ocean as a marine engineer.

1. A trouble is a trouble, and the general idea, in the country, is to treat it as such, rather than to snatch the knotted cords from the hand of God and deal out murderous blows.

.   .   .   .

It is extraordinary how many emotional storms one may weather in safety if one is ballasted with ever so little gold.

.   .   .   .

The world belongs to the enthusiast who keeps cool.

.   .   .   .

Terrible and sublime thought, that every moment is supreme for some man or woman, every hour the apotheosis of some passion!   *Casuals of the Sea*

2. High-brow communists affect vast interest in pictures of machinery as art. They discover aesthetic qualities in a photograph of a broken crankshaft or the gear-wheels of a power press. A couple of screws lying on a mirror will send them into toothy ecstacies of appreciation.   *A Six-Hour Shift*

3. Most of our nautical fiction seems to be caulked with hokum . . . it is almost impossible to get Americans to view the life of a seafaring man save as a chapter out of Jack London's *Sea Wolf* or some equally virile and odious fiction.

More Harbours of Memory

FRANKLIN DELANO ROOSEVELT (1882–1945)

THE thirty-first President's long term in office—(a present Constitutional amendment has since ruled a maximum of two consecutive terms) gave him national leadership under two historic circumstances, the Depression and World War II. Few men have had such a remarkable faculty for stating tersely epigrammatic thoughts reflecting current popular feeling. Though Presidential speeches are often the work of many hands, the Roosevelt "touch" was apparent.

1. Any government, like any family, can for a year spend a little more than it earns. But you and I know that a continuance of that habit means the poorhouse.

Speech, 1932

2. . . . the only thing we have to fear is fear itself.

.   .   .   .

In the field of world policy I would dedicate this nation to the policy of the good neighbor.

.   .   .   .

For the trust reposed in me I will return the courage and devotion that befits the time. I can do no less. We face the arduous days that lie before us in the warm courage of national unity; with the clear consciousness of seeking old and precious moral values; with the clean satisfaction that comes from the stern performance of duty by old and young alike. We aim at the assurance of a rounded and permanent national life. We do not distrust the future of essential democracy. *First Inaugural Address, 1933*

3. This generation of Americans has a rendezvous with destiny. *Speech accepting renomination 1939*

4. A Conservative is a man with two perfectly good legs who, however, has never learned to walk. *Speech, 1939*

5. With confidence in our armed forces, with unbounded determination of our people, we will gain the inevitable triumph. So help us God. *Speech, December 9, 1941*

6. The only limit to our realization of tomorrow will be our doubts of today. Let us move forward with strong and active faith. *Undelivered Jefferson Day Speech, 1945*

(ANNA) ELEANOR ROOSEVELT (1884–1962)

THE wife of the thirty-first President, achieved prominence as a writer and speaker in so many fields that she has an individual claim to fame. She rose to her greatest height, however, when, as a delegate to the United Nations, she expressed its meaning to her.

Without the United Nations our country would walk alone, ruled by fear, instead of confidence and hope. *Speech, 1952*

HARRY S. TRUMAN (1884–   )

THE thirty-second President has been noted for the pungent wisecrack rather than for lasting quotations, but he spoke thoughtfully and truthfully when his successor, President Eisenhower, was bedeviled by a Democrat-controlled Congress. Mr. Truman resolutely admonished his own party colleagues to co-operate.

Our government cannot function properly unless the President is master in his own house.   *Speech, 1954*

RING (RINGOLD WILMER) LARDNER (1885–1933)

LARDNER carved out a special niche for himself as a writer first of sports stories and afterward as a humorist with acid in his pen. In 1916 he became famous with his collection of short stories entitled, *You Know Me, Al*, but within a few years was more noted for his satirical short stories debunking the sports "heroes" of his day.

1. Beyond Those Billboards Lies New Jersey.

Title of Article

2. Mother set facing the front end of the train, as it makes her giddy to ride backwards. I set facing her, which does not affect me.   *The Golden Honeymoon*

3. A good many young writers make the mistake of enclosing a stamped, self-addressed envelope, big enough for the manuscript to come back in. This is too much of a temptation to the editor.

Personally I have found it a good scheme to not even sign my name to the story, and when I have got it sealed up in its envelope and stamped and addressed, I take it to some town where I don't live and mail it from there. The editor has no idea who wrote the story, so how can he send it back?

How to Write Short Stories

SINCLAIR LEWIS (1885–1951)

THE phrases "Main Street" and "Babbitt," now part of the American vocabulary, were Lewis's literary inventions. Two of the quotations here—one from a letter declining a Pulitzer Prize ($500) and the other from his speech accepting later the Nobel prize (about $50,-000) for literature give us some idea of this controversial man whose acidulous comments over a long period cost him probably as much in esteem from his colleagues as he gained in royalties and a certain public adulation for his writings.

1. Not only Gopher Prairie, but ten thousand towns from Albany to San Diego . . . not a dozen buildings which suggested that, in the fifty years of Gopher Prairie's existence, the citizens had realized that it was either desirable or possible to make this, their common home, amusing or attractive.   *Main Street*

2. Between the Pulitzer Prizes, the American Academy of Arts and Letters and its training-school the National Institute of Arts and Letters, amateur boards of censorship, and the inquisition of earnest literary ladies, every compulsion is put upon writers to become safe, polite, obedient, and sterile. In protest, I declined election to the National Institute of Arts and Letters some years ago, and now I must decline the Pulitzer Prize.

I invite other writers to consider the fact that by accepting the prizes and approval of these vague institutions, we are admitting their authority, publicly confirming them as the final judges of literary excellence, and I inquire whether any prize is worth that subservience.   *Public letter declining the Pulitzer Prize, 1926*

3. To a true-blue professor of literature in an American university, literature is not something that a plain human being, living today, painfully sits down to produce. No; it is something dead; it is something magically produced by superhuman beings who must, if they are to be regarded as artists at all, have died at least one hundred years before the diabolical invention of the typewriter. To any authentic don, there is something slightly repulsive in the thought that literature could be created by any ordinary human being, still to be seen walking the streets, wearing quite commonplace trousers and coat and looking not so unlike a chauffeur or a farmer. Our American professors like their literature clear and cold and pure and very dead.

Address accepting the Nobel Prize for
Literature, Stockholm, 1930

4. That nation is proudest and noblest and most exalted which has the greatest number of really great men.

EZRA LOOMIS POUND (1885–   )

POUND wrote many years ago that poems should be criticised, rather than poets who wrote them. Could he have anticipated the difficulties and criticism that beseiged him at the height of his fame as an international poet? (He was indicted for treason for broadcasting Fascist propaganda from Italy during the Second World War and was adjudged insane in 1945.) As a poet he won wide recognition before he was thirty, both for original works and for translations from the Chinese and Latin. His highly intellectual but lyric poetry has enjoyed an enormous influence in this century.

1. It is only after long experience that most men are able to define a thing in terms of its own genus, painting as painting, writing as writing. You can spot the bad critic when he starts by discussing the poet and not the poem.

. . . .

There is no reason why the same man should like the same book at 18 and at 48.

. . . .

Men do not understand books until they have had a certain amount of life, or at any rate no man understands a deep book, until he has seen and lived at least part of its contents.

A B C of Reading

2. Go, my songs, to the lonely and the unsatisfied,
   Go also to the nerve-wracked, go to the enslaved-by-convention,
   Bear to them my contempt for their oppressors.

Commission

LOUIS UNTERMEYER (1885–   )

THIS poet, critic, translator, scholar and lecturer whose poems constitute his best-known landmark ran counter to most of the rules governing the lives of great literary figures. His formal education ended with high school, when he went into the family's jewelry business, and he was thirty-eight years old when he resigned from his prosperous executive positions to study and write.

1. From compromise and things half done,
       Keep me with stern and stubborn pride;
   And when at last the fight is won,
       God, keep me still unsatisfied.

Prayer

2. May nothing evil cross this door,
       And may ill fortune never pry
   About these windows; may the roar
       And rains go by.

Prayer for This House

ZOË AKINS (1886–1958)

AS poet and writer, Miss Akins has trod the "quiet path," never dramatic or sensational, but voicing a loving appreciation of life.

1. So much do I love wandering,
       So much I love the sea and sky,
   That it will be a piteous thing
       In one small grave to lie. . . .

The Wanderer

2. Nothing seems so tragic to one who is old as the death of one who is young, and this alone proves that life is a good thing.

WILLIAM ROSE BENÉT (1886–1950)

THE older brother of Stephen Vincent Benét was a man of many literary accomplishments. He was a distinguished editor of several important magazines including the *Century* and the *Saturday Review of Literature,* which he helped to found, author of essays and novels and ultimately winner, in 1942, of the Pulitzer Prize for poetry.

1. Who writes poetry imbibes honey from the poisoned lips of life.

. . . .

I know some force is mighty, some force I cannot reach,
I know that words are said to me that are not said with
    speech.
My heart has learnt a lesson that I can never teach.
Only this I know, that I am overtaken
By a swifter runner Whose breath is never shaken,
That I follow on his pace, and that round me, as I waken,
Are the headlands of home and the blue sea swinging
And the flowers of the valleys their fresh scents flinging
And the prophets and the poets, with their singing—with
    their singing!

Man Possessed

2. Jesse James was a two-gun man.

. . . .

Roll on, Missouri!

. . . .

In seven states he cut up dadoes.
He's gone with the buffer an' the desperadoes.

Jesse James: American Myth

3. You are to me what the bowstring is to the shaft,
Speeding my purposes aloft and aflame and afar.

Dedication

4. You cannot slay yourself in me,
Nor I—to all eternity—
Destroy my truest self in you.
All that our ingrate thought will do,
All senseless wounds we give and take,
Are powerless, for the other's sake.

We Ask No Shield

VAN WYCK BROOKS (1886–1963)

NEW Jersey born and Harvard educated, Brooks, with publication in 1936 of his Pulitzer prize-winning book, *The Flowering of New England,* won recognition as one of the leading interpreters of the Puritan influence on American development. His first book on the subject had been published in 1909; subsequent books develop the theme. At the time he died, it was noted that he had read in full every source he had mentioned in his voluminous work.

1. His wife not only edited his works but edited him.

The Ordeal of Mark Twain

2. As against having beautiful workshops, studios, etc., one writes best in a cellar on a rainy day.

Epigrams

3. Emerson advised his fellow-townsmen to manufacture school-teachers and make them the best in the world.

The Flowering of New England

JOYCE KILMER (1886–1918)

THIS poet, immortalized by his poem, "Trees," was killed in World War I, a tragic waste of what might have proved a major talent. He was already famous as an interpreter of simple human values seen through inspired eyes.

1. There is no peace to be taken
     With poets who are young,
   For they worry about the wars to be fought
     And the songs that must be sung.

Old Poets

2. A house that has echoed a baby's laugh and held up his stumbling feet,

Is the saddest sight, when it's left alone, that ever your
   eyes could meet.

The House with Nobody in It

3. For nothing keeps a poet
      In his high singing mood
   Like unappeasable hunger
      For unattainable food.

Apology

4. It is stern work, it is perilous work to thrust your hand in
      the sun
   And pull out a spark of immortal flame to warm the hearts
      of men.

The Proud Poet

ALEXANDER WOOLLCOTT (1887–1943)

NO literary and dramatic critic of the twentieth century has yet exceeded in popular reputation Woollcott, who not only wrote criticism but took it "to the air" with enormous effect on public taste in his weekly radio series, "The Town Crier," which continued as a popular feature for eleven years from 1929 through 1940.

1. All the things I really like to do are either immoral, illegal or fattening.

2. The attitude of the professional player toward the amateurs is best summed up in a raffish story they delight in telling on all occasions. It begins with a touching picture of an old broken-down tragedian sharing a park bench with a bedraggled and unappetizing street-walker. "Ah, Madame," says the tragedian, *"quelle ironie!* The two oldest professions in the world—ruined by amateurs."

The Knock at the Stage-Door

3. Beerbohm Tree said what we have all wanted to say of the extra women in nearly every throne-room and ball-room and school-room scene since the theatre began. "Ladies," said Tree,

peering at them plaintively through his monocle, "just a little more virginity, if you don't mind." *Capsule Criticism*

HEYWOOD CAMPBELL BROUN (1888–1939)

IN his relatively short life the physically enormous Broun produced his world-famous columns in the New York *World* under the heading, "It Seems to Me," critical, informative, often acidulous, but always thought-provoking and interesting.

1. The ability to make love frivolously is the chief characteristic which distinguishes human beings from the beasts.

· · · ·

"Trees" (if I have the name right) is one of the most annoying pieces of verse within my knowledge. The other one is Kipling's "If," with a third place reserved for Henley's "Invictus."

"Trees" maddens me, because it contains the most insincere line ever written by mortal man. Surely the Kilmer tongue must not have been very far from the Kilmer cheek when he wrote, "Poems are made by fools like me."

· · · ·

It is a good trick when a writer can go out and set down with accuracy some living being whom he has observed with fidelity. He holds the mirror up to Nature. But that is not the furthest reach of literature. . . . Life is a copycat and can be bullied into following the master artist who bids it come to heel.

· · · ·

I have known people to stop and buy an apple on the corner and then walk away as if they had solved the whole unemployment problem. *It Seems to Me*

2. A newspaper is a rule unto itself. It has a soul for salvation or damnation. The intangibles of a newspaper are the men and women who make it. A newspaper can neither rise nor fall below its staff.

EUGENE O'NEILL (1888-1953)

THERE are few who would dispute Eugene O'Neill's reputation as the greatest playwright in the field of tragedy in his generation. Son of James O'Neill, the actor, he spent boyhood travelling with his father's company. In turn laborer, seaman, prospector and newspaperman, he later became associated with the Provincetown Players and going on to popular as well as artistic success. He won three Pulitzer prizes, and in 1936 was awarded the Nobel Prize in Literature.

1. Dat ole davil, sea. *Anna Christie*

2. For de little stealin' dey gits you in jail soon or late. For de big stealin' dey makes you emperor and puts you in de Hall o' Fame when you croaks. If dey's one thing I learns in ten years on de Pullman cars listenin' to de white quality talk, it's dat same fact.
The Emperor Jones

3. He couldn't design a cathedral without it looking like the First Supernatural Bank. *The Great God Brown*

4. Our lives are merely strange dark interludes in the electrical display of God the Father! *Strange Interlude*

ALAN SEEGER (1888-1916)

FIGHTING with the French Army, Seeger was a casualty of World War I long before his own country was officially involved. His own "rendezvous with death" came before he fulfilled his promise.

2. I have a rendezvous with Death
   At some disputed barricade,
   When Spring comes back with rustling shade
   And apple-blossoms fill the air.

   .   .   .   .

   When Spring trips north again this year,
   And I to my pledged word am true,

I shall not fail that rendezvous.

I Have a Rendezvous With Death

CONRAD AIKEN (1889–   )

GEORGIA-BORN and Harvard educated, this renowned poet, novelist and critic, began his literary successes with a book of poems published only three years after his graduation from college in 1911.

1. Music I heard with you was more than music,
   And bread I broke with you was more than bread.
   "Music I Heard"

2. Ice is the silent language of the peak;
   and fire the silent language of the star.
   And in the Human Heart

3. All lovely things will have an ending,
   All lovely things will fade and die,
   And youth, that's now so bravely spending,
   Will beg a penny by and by.
   "All Lovely Things"

4. How shall we praise the magnificence of the dead,
   The great man humbled, the haughty brought to dust?
   Is there a horn we should not blow as proudly
   For the meanest of us all, who creeps his days,
   Guarding his heart from blows, to die obscurely?
   Tetélestai

HERVEY ALLEN (1889–1949)

THE success of Allen's novel *Anthony Adverse* has all but obscured recollection of Allen's other notable work as biographer and poet. *Anthony Adverse* appeared in 1933; it was to become the longest and best-selling novel that had yet appeared on the American scene.

1. Grow up as soon as you can. It pays. The only time you really live fully is from thirty to sixty.

· · · ·

The young are slaves to dreams; the old servants of regrets.

· · · ·

What is even a wise book but a blast from the lungs made visible to the eyes?   *Anthony Adverse*

WALTER LIPPMANN (1889–   )

AT this writing, Lippmann is one of the most respected and widely read of political columnists and commentators. His vigorous career began publicly as President Wilson's Assistant Secretary of War who helped draft resolutions at the Versailles Peace Conference.

The politician says, "I will give you what you want." The statesman says, "What you think you want is this. What it is possible for you to get is that. What you really want, therefore, is the following. . . ."   *A Preface to Morals*

JAMES J. WALKER (1889–1940)

WALKER will be remembered, if at all, as the epitome of the wise-cracking, irresponsible, smooth character of the "gay twenties." Mayor of New York early enough to celebrate his fortieth birthday in office, the scandal of corruption in office forced his resignation in 1932.

1. I never knew a girl who was ruined by a book.
            Debate on censorship in New York Senate
2. Some folks call me the "night mayor" of New York.

FRANCIS CARDINAL SPELLMAN (1889–)

THIS benign prince of the Roman Catholic Church is one of the most popular men of his following. Since the Korean War Cardinal Spellman has spent every Christmas with one group or another of American soldiers assigned to lonely outposts abroad.

Pray as if everything depended on God, and work as if everything depended upon man.

MARC (MARCUS COOK) CONNELLY (1890–)

AUTHOR of many plays and movies which have brought him overwhelming success, Connelly reached his height of popularity with *The Green Pastures,* a Pulitzer Prize play, 1930.

Gangway for de Lawd God Jehovah!

. . . .

How about cleanin' up de whole mess of 'em and sta'tin' all over ag'in wid some new kind of animal?

. . . .

Even bein' Gawd ain't a bed of roses. *The Green Pastures*

DWIGHT DAVID EISENHOWER (1890–)

THE thirty-third President, former commander of Allied Forces in Europe and president of Columbia University and one of the most honored men, edited his biography in *Who's Who in America* down to a scant two inches, with no mention of his decorations.

1. Destiny has laid upon our country the responsibility of the free world's leadership.

.   .   .   .

Whatever America hopes to bring to pass in the world must first come to pass in the heart of America.

Inaugural Address, 1954

2. Freedom from fear and injustice and oppression will be ours only in the measure that men who value such freedom are ready to sustain its possession—to defend it against every thrust from within and without.

CHRISTOPHER MORLEY
(1890–1957)

EDITOR, novelist and poet, Morley's first distinction came as a student when he was awarded a Rhodes scholarship. He was one of the founders and editor of the *Saturday Review of Literature* and twice revised modern editions of Bartlett's *Familiar Quotations*.

1. Why do they put the Gideon Bibles only in the bedrooms, where it's usually too late, and not in the barroom downstairs?

2. She [New York] is the only city whose lovers live always in a mood of wonder and expectancy. There are others where one may sink peacefully, contentedly into the life of the town, affectionate and understanding of its ways. But she, the woman city, who is bold enough to say he understands her?

3. A human being: an ingenious assemblage of portable plumbing.

.   .   .   .

How great a bonfire the savages of New York kindle for their evening meal!

Human Being

4. Poetry comes with anger, hunger and dismay; it does not often visit groups of citizens sitting down to be literary together.

.   .   .   .

April prepares her green traffic light and the world thinks Go.

John Mistletoe

ARCHIBALD MacLEISH (1892–   )

FEW poets have had such varied careers as MacLeish. At various times Librarian of Congress, Assistant Secretary of State, government official in World War II, and professor of Rhetoric at Harvard University, MacLeish first won fame and the Pulitzer Prize in 1932 for his narrative poem "Conquistador." Later two more Pulitzer Prizes were to be his: one for his *Collected Poems, 1917–1952,* and the latest for his play, *J.B.* in 1958.

1. Beauty is that Medusa's head
   Which men go armed to seek and sever.
   It is most deadly when most dead,
   And dead will stare and sting forever.

   Beauty

2. A poem should not mean
   But be.

   Ars Poetica

3. The world was always yours; you would not take it.

   Speech to a Crowd

EDNA ST. VINCENT MILLAY (1892–1950)

ANOTHER Pulitzer Prize winner, Miss Millay (later Mrs. Eugen Jan Boissevain) astounded the literary world by the publication of her first volume of poetry the year she was graduated from Vassar, 1917. A writer of short stories and verse-plays as well, her lyrics have been compared by critics with the best of the Elizabethan romantics.

1. And what are you that, missing you,
   I should be kept awake

      As many nights as there are days
        With weeping for your sake?

The Philosopher

2. I drank at every vine,
    The last was like the first.
I came upon no wine
    So wonderful as thirst.

Feast

3. My candle burns at both ends;
    It will not last the night;
But, ah, my foes, and, oh, my friends—
It gives a lovely light!

A Fig from Thistles: First Fig

4. Spring rides no horses down the hill.
But comes on foot, a goose girl still.
And all the loveliest things there be
Come simply, so, it seems to me.
If ever I said, in grief or pride,
I tired of honest things, I lied.

The Goose Girl

5. My heart is warm with the friends I make,
    And better friends I'll not be knowing;
Yet there isn't a train I wouldn't take,
    No matter where it's going.

Travel

WENDELL L. WILLKIE (1892–1944)

FEW men have lived as vigorously as this Indiana-born-and-educated man who in his brief life was a successful corporation lawyer and industrialist before he "bucked" the Republican Party organization to win nomination for the Presidency in 1940. He lost to Franklin D. Roosevelt, but polled 22,000,000 votes in doing so.

1. One world   *Title of his first book*
2. Our American unity must be forged between the ideas of

the opposition and the practices and policies of the administration.
Speech, 1940

3. American liberty is a religion. It is a thing of the spirit.
It is an aspiration on the part of the people for not alone a free life
but a better life; . . . . *Speech, 1941*

RAYMOND FERNAND LOEWY (1893–)

THIS French-born engineer and industrial designer has probably exerted as much influence as any individual on modern developments in his field. He once was quoted as saying that two shapes that could not be improved were those of the egg and the Coca-Cola bottle.

New York is simply a distillation of the United States, the most of everything, the conclusive proof that there is an American civilization. New York is casual, intellectual, subtle, effective and devastatingly witty. But her sophisticated appearance is the thinnest of veneers. Beneath it there is power, virility, determination and a sense of destiny.

ANITA LOOS (1893–)

MISS Loos (Mrs. John Emerson) has enjoyed a career studded with successes as a writer of plays and motion picture scripts. She will be best remembered for her 1925 play and movie immortalizing blondes.

Diamonds are a girl's best friend.
Gentlemen Prefer Blondes

DOROTHY PARKER (1893–)

THE popularity of Miss Parker's (Mrs. Alan Campbell) satirically impish verse has often obscured her other and substantial claims to note as a writer of short stories, plays and critical essays.

1. Where the man could ease a heart
Like a satin gown?

The Satin Dress

2. Four be the things I am wiser to know:
Idleness, sorrow, a friend, and a foe.

. . . .

Four be the things I'd been better without:
Love, curiosity, freckles, and doubt.

Inventory

3. Men seldom make passes
At girls who wear glasses.

News Item

4. Women and elephants never forget.

Ballade of Unfortunate Mammals

WESTBROOK PEGLER (1894–   )

A former sports writer of the Chicago school, Pegler turned to writing a successful column devoted to exposing the chicanery in professional sports, and later became one of the most controversial and successful columnists, who would investigate anything and everything that caught his critical eye.

1. I am a member of the rabble in good standing.

The Lynching Story

2. After a quiet study of the rules and tools of civilized table warfare your correspondent has decided that the French combine the greatest simplicity with the best results.

The Frenchman, like the old Scotch golfer, endeavors to do what there is to be done without superfluous weapons or fancy gestures. He sits down, ties his napkin behind his ears, picks up a knife and fork and goes to work with admirable directness. He dunks his bread in the juice of the snail, he chases fragments of steak and gravy with a piece of crust, he licks his fingers, says, "Ah!" and gets fed. *France in One Easy Lesson*

F. SCOTT FITZGERALD
(1896–1940)

THE psychology of Fitzgerald as man and writer is presently a favorite theme of the critics. In his brilliant career, cut tragically short, this spokesman of the "Lost Generation" produced a wealth of short stories and novels, including *The Great Gatsby*.

In a real dark night of the soul it is always three o'clock in the morning.

WILLIAM FAULKNER (1897–1962)

FAULKNER was a giant among his peers. His major writings, noted for their highly individualistic style, deal mainly with the Deep South, the mores of which Faulkner examines in his mythic microcosm, Yoknapatawpha County. His forty-year writing career won him the Nobel Prize in Literature, and on his death in 1962 he was awarded this accolade from the late President Kennedy: "Since Henry James, no writer has left behind such a vast and enduring monument to the strength of American literature."

I decline to accept the end of man. . . . I believe that man will not merely endure; he will prevail. He is immortal not because he alone among creatures has an inexhaustible voice, but because he has a soul, a spirit capable of compassion and sacrifice and endurance. *Accepting Nobel Prize in Literature, 1950*

STEPHEN VINCENT BENÉT
(1898–1943)

THIS younger brother of William Rose Benét carved his own niche in the world of literature. The masterwork of this poet and short story writer is considered to be "John Brown's Body," a lengthy drama in verse that sharply in-creased the popular interest in poetry.

1. He could fiddle all the bugs off a sweet-potato-vine.
   The Mountain Whippoorwill
2. There were human beings aboard the Mayflower,
     Not merely ancestors.
   Western Star
3. The ants find kingdoms in a foot of ground.
   John Brown's Body
4. I have fallen in love with American names,
   The sharp names that never get fat,
   The snakeskin-titles of mining-claims,
   The plumed war-bonnet of Medicine Hat,
   Tucson and Deadwood and Lost Mule Flat.

   .   .   .   .

   I shall not rest quiet in Montparnasse.
   I shall not lie easy at Winchelsea.
   You may bury my body in Sussex grass,
   You may bury my tongue at Champmedy.
   I shall not be there. I shall rise and pass.
   Bury my heart at Wounded Knee.
   American Names

LOUIS ADAMIC (1899–1951)

BORN in Blato, Slovenia [now in Yugoslavia], Adamic came to the United States at the age of 14, edu-cated himself, and became through his writings a great expositor of the American Opportunity.

There is a certain blend of courage, integrity, character and principle which has no satisfactory dictionary name but has been called different things at different times in different countries. Our American name for it is "guts." *A Study in Courage*

ELWYN BROOKS (E.B.) WHITE (1899–)

A brilliant descriptive writer with a strong sense of humor, White for years contributed the "Talk of the Town," to the *New Yorker* magazine. At this writing he continues to delight an army of readers.

1. To date New York has shown nothing but progress. Hopefully we wait the first signs of decadence—partial decadence being the only condition under which anybody can exist with any degree of grace or civility.   *Here Is New York*

2. The critic leaves at curtain fall
     To find, in starting to review it,
  He scarcely saw the play at all
     For watching his reaction to it.

Critic

JOHN MASON BROWN (1900–)

AS drama critic, editor of a major book club and general commentator, Brown also found time to publish in 1963, after years of preliminary work, an extraordinary collection of reminiscences—virtually a history of the modern American theater. Yet few would dispute that these spoken words are his finest.

I am sick and tired of the snivelers, the defeated, and the whiners. I am sick and tired of being expected to believe that ugliness is beauty, that melancholy is man's sole pleasure, that delinquency is delight, that laughter is something to be ashamed of.

.   .   .   .

I have lived long enough to be battered by the realities of life and not too long to be downed by them.   *Speech, 1958*

ADLAI EWING STEVENSON
(1900–   )

TWICE an unsuccessful candidate for the Presidency, this California-born former Governor of Illinois, at the time of the compilation of this work, was chief of the mission to the United Nations.

1. Let's talk sense to the American people.   *Speech, 1952*

2. If the pursuit of peace is both old and new, it is also both complicated and simple. It is complicated, because it has to do with people, and nothing in this universe baffles man as much as himself.   *Speech, 1952*

3. Let us present once more the true face of America—warm and modest and friendly, dedicated to the welfare of all mankind, and demanding nothing except a chance for all to live and let live, to grow and govern as they wish, free from interference, free from intimidation, free from fear.   *Speech, 1955*

4. To act coolly, intelligently and prudently in perilous circumstances is the test of a man and also a nation.   *Speech, 1955*

CHARLES AUGUSTUS LINDBERGH
(1902–   )

WHEN a twenty-five-year-old pilot, in 1927, flew alone from New York to Paris in a single-engined airplane named "The Spirit of St. Louis," he became a legend. "Lindy" always insisted, however, that his fame be shared with his plane (now in the Smithsonian Institution.)

We (that's my ship and I) . . .   *Describing his flight*

OGDEN NASH (1902–   )

TO be a financially successful poet and a member of the American Academy of Arts and Letters is a very rare accomplishment. The seeming easiness with which Nash slips into his clever (though at times outrageous) puns-in-verse should not detract from his genuine gift for lyric and for biting satire, both difficult arts to master.

1. I think that I shall never see
A billboard lovely as a tree.
Indeed, unless the billboards fall,
I'll never see a tree at all.

Song of the Open Road

2. Candy
Is dandy
But liquor
Is quicker.

Reflection on Ice-Breaking

3. I wonder if the citizens of New York will ever get sufficiently wroth
To remember that Tammany cooks spoil the broth.

Speculative Reflection

4. This is the sum total of Thanksgiving lore:
Not to be thankful until you're tired of what you're being thankful for.

A Short Outline of Thanksgiving

5. The old men know when an old man dies.

Old Men

JOHN ERNST STEINBECK (1902–   )

THE "list" of this prolific author is too lengthy to be included in any summary biography such as this. It was Steinbeck who, with his *Grapes of Wrath,* put the term "Okies" into the common American vocabulary.

There was some irony, however, in the fact that his winning of the Nobel Prize for Literature occurred simultaneously with the publication of his whimsical *Travels with Charley,* for his other works have been far more ambitious in scope.

New York is an ugly city, a dirty city. Its climate is a scandal, its politics are used to frighten children, its traffic is madness, its competition is murderous. But there is one thing about it—once you have lived in New York and it has become your home, no place else is good enough.

J. ROBERT OPPENHEIMER (1904–)

AS a physicist, Oppenheimer directed the science laboratory at Los Alamos, where the first atom bomb was developed; as an educator he since has become Director of the Institute for Advanced Study, at Princeton, New Jersey. But aside from these honors he is a student of man, as he eloquently showed in these excerpts from the address he was invited to deliver at the closing session of Columbia University's bicentennial celebration in 1954.

Our knowledge separates us as well as it unites; our orders disintegrate as well as bind; our art brings us together and sets us apart.

. . . .

Both the man of science and the man of action live always at the edge of mystery, surrounded by it.

. . . .

In the material sciences these are and have been, and are most surely likely to continue to be heroic days.

. . . .

We know too much for one man to know much.

THOMAS MERTON (1915–)

FROM this unique figure in American literature, a French-born, British-educated former professor of English in American colleges, has issued a steady stream of books—notable ones—since 1944. His "home" is the Trappist Abbey of Our Lady of Gethsemani, in Kentucky, where since 1941 he has advanced from novice, to priest, to Master of Novices while continuing a steady writing career.

"I look forward to a great future for America -- a future in which our country will match its military strength with our moral restraint, its wealth with our wisdom, its power with our purposes. I look forward to an America which will not be afraid of grace and beauty ... which will reward achievement in business or statecraft... which commands respect throughout the world not only for its strength but for its civilization as well."

Spoken at the dedication of
The Robert Frost Library,
Amherst College,
Amherst, Massachusetts
October 26, 1963

J.R Rosen
Boston

By the reading of Scripture I am so renewed that all nature seems renewed around me and with me. The sky seems to be a pure, a cooler blue, the trees a deeper green. . . . The whole world is charged with the glory of God and I feel fire and music . . . under my feet.   *Quoted in The New York Times, 1963*

JOHN FITZGERALD KENNEDY (1917–1963)

THE first President of the United States born in the twentieth century, and the youngest ever to be elected, compressed within forty-six years a striking career that had not yet had time to flower when an assassin struck him down in Dallas, Texas, on November 22, 1963.

Though his abilities as President overshadowed his other talents, it is to be remembered that he wrote two notable books, *While England Slept* and *Profiles in Courage*. The latter won him a Pulitzer Prize for Literature. As a practitioner and admirer of the arts, he personally invited Robert Frost to participate in his Inaugural Ceremonies, elevated the fields of science, the theater and literature to a high place in White House circles. As President he gave vigorous lead-ership to the cause of political and social reform—causes that often aroused controversy but were, as is firmly believed, in the country's best interest.

On John F. Kennedy's death, President Johnson paid this tribute in proclaiming November 25 a day of national mourning:

"He upheld the faith of our Fathers, which is freedom for all men. He broadened the frontiers of that faith, and backed it with the energy and courage which are the mark of the nation that he led.

"A man of wisdom, strength and peace, he molded and moved the power of our Nation in the service of a world of growing liberty and order. All who love freedom will mourn his death."

Johnson spoke for the nation.

1. To those nations who would make themselves our adversary, we offer not a pledge but a request; that both sides begin anew the quest for peace, before the dark powers of destruction unleashed by science engulf all humanity in planned or accidental self-destruction.

.   .   .   .

So let us begin anew—remembering on both sides that civility is not a sign of weakness, and sincerity is always subject to proof. Let us never negotiate out of fear. But let us never fear to negotiate.

．　　　．　　　．　　　．

And so, my fellow Americans: ask not what your country can do for you—ask what you can do for your country. My fellow citizens of the world: ask not what America will do for you, but what together we can do for the freedom of man.

Inaugural Address, 1960

2. On the Presidential coat of arms, the American eagle holds in his right talon an olive branch, while in his left he holds a bundle of arrows. We intend to give equal attention to both.

State of the Union Message, 1961

3. Together we shall save our planet or together we shall perish in its flames. . . . It is . . . our intention to challenge the Soviet Union, not to an arms race, but to a peace race; to advance step by step, stage by stage, until general and complete disarmament has actually been achieved. *On disarmament, 1962*

4. All free men, wherever they may live, are citizens of Berlin. And therefore, as a free man, I take pride in the words, *"Ich bin ein Berliner* (I am a Berliner).*"*　　*At the Berlin Wall, 1963*

5. [The] result of continued Federal legislative inaction will continue, if not increase, racial strife—causing the leadership of both sides to pass from the hands of reasonable and responsible men to the purveyors of hate and violence.

Speech on Civil Rights, 1963

6. When power leads man toward arrogance, poetry reminds him of his limitations. When power narrows the area of man's concern, poetry reminds him of the richness and diversity of his existence. When power corrupts, poetry cleanses.

At Amherst College, honoring Robert Frost, 1963

ALPHABETICAL LISTING OF AUTHORS AND SOURCES

ADAMIC, LOUIS, author (1899–1951)
ADAMS, FRANKLIN PIERCE, columnist (1881–1960)
ADAMS, HENRY, author (1838–1918)
ADAMS, JOHN, President (1735–1826)
ADAMS, JOHN QUINCY, President (1767–1848)
ADAMS, SAMUEL, patriot (1722–1803)
ADDAMS, JANE, social worker (1860–1935)
ADE, GEORGE, humorist (1866–1944)
AIKEN, CONRAD, poet (1889–   )
AKINS, ZOË, writer (1886–1958)
ALCOTT, AMOS BRONSON, educator (1799–1888)
ALCOTT, LOUISA MAY, author (1832–1888)
ALDRICH, THOMAS BAILEY, author-poet (1836–1907)
ALDRIDGE, IRA FREDERICK, tragedian (1805–1867)
ALLEN, ELIZABETH AKERS, poet (1832–1911)
ALLEN, HERVEY, author (1889–1949)
ALLEN, JAMES LANE, author (1849–1925)
ALLSTON, WASHINGTON, painter (1779–1843)
AMES, FISHER, statesman (1758–1808)
ANDERSON, HAROLD MACDONALD, editor (1876–1940)
ANSPACHER, LOUIS KAUFMAN, sociologist (1878–1947)
ANTHONY, SUSAN BROWNELL, Suffragette (1820–1906)
ANTIN, MARY, author (1881–1949)
ATHERTON, GERTRUDE F. (HORN), author (1857–1948)

BACKER, CARL LOTUS, philosopher-economist (1873–1945)
BALLOU, HOSEA, clergyman (1771–1852)
BANGS, JOHN KENDRICK, author (1862–1922)
BARLOW, JOEL, poet-patriot (1754–1812)
BARNUM, PHINEAS T., circus impresario (1810–1891)
BARRYMORE, ETHEL, actress (1879–1959)

ROOSEVELT, (ANNA) ELEANOR (1884–1962)
ROOSEVELT, FRANKLIN DELANO, President (1882–1945)
ROOSEVELT, THEODORE, President (1858–1919)
ROOT, GEORGE FREDERIC, composer (1820–1895)

SALM, MADAME DE, actress (1840– ?)
SANBORN, FRANKLIN BENJAMIN, editor (1831–1917)
SANDBURG, CARL, author-poet (1878–   )
SANTAYANA, GEORGE, philosopher (1863–1952)
SAXE, JOHN GODFREY, poet-humorist (1816–1887)
SCHURZ, CARL, editor-statesman (1829–1906)
SCOLLARD, CLINTON, poet (1860–1932)
SEEGAR, ALAN, poet (1888–1916)
SEWARD, WILLIAM HENRY, statesman (1801–1872)
SHAW, HENRY WHEELER (See Josh Billings)
SHERMAN, WILLIAM TECUMSEH, army officer (1820–1891)
SHERMAN, SIDNEY, army officer (1805–1873)
SIMMS, WILLIAM GILMORE, novelist (1806–1870)
SMITH, ALFRED E., governor (1873–1944)
SMITH, ELIZABETH OAKES, poet (1806–1893)
SMITH, SAMUEL FRANCIS, poet (1808–1895)
SMITH, LOGAN PEARSALL, author (1865–1946)
SPELLMAN, FRANCIS CARDINAL (1889–   )
SPRAGUE, CHARLES, banker-poet (1791–1875)
STANTON, CHARLES E., army officer (1859–1933)
STEIN, GERTRUDE, poet (1874–1946)
STEINBECK, JOHN, author (1902–   )
STEVENSON, ADLAI EWING, statesman (1900–   )
STOWE, HARRIET BEECHER, author (1811–1896)
STRUNSKY, SIMEON, author (1879–1948)
SUMNER, CHARLES, statesman (1811–1874)

TABB, JOHN BANNISTER, poet (1845–1909)
TARKINGTON, (NEWTON) BOOTH, author (1869–1946)
TATTNALL, JOSEPH, naval officer (1795–1871)
TAYLOR, BERT LESTON, columnist (1866–1921)
TAYLOR, BAYARD, diplomat-poet (1825–1878)
THANKSGIVING, FIRST AMERICAN PROCLAMATION (June 20, 1676)
THAYER, ERNEST LAWRENCE, writer (1863–1940)
THOMPSON, WILLIAM HENRY, poet, (1848–1918)
THOREAU, HENRY DAVID, author-naturalist (1817–1862)
THORPE, ROSE HARTWICK, poet (1850–1939)
TILTON, THEODORE, journalist (1835–1907)
TRUMAN, HARRY S., President (1884–   )
TWAIN, MARK (See Samuel Clemens)
TWEED, WILLIAM M., politician (1823–1878)

UNTERMEYER, LOUIS, poet (1885–   )

VANDERBILT, WILLIAM HENRY, financier (1821–1885)
VANDIVER, WILLIAM DUNCAN (1854–1932)
VAN DYKE, HENRY, clergyman (1852–1933)
VEBLEN, THORSTEIN, teacher (1857–1929)
VEST, GEORGE GRAHAM, senator (1830–1904)

WALKER, JAMES J., New York Mayor (1881–1946)
WALLACE, WILLIAM ROSS, poet (1819–1881)
WARD, ARTEMUS (Charles Farrar Browne), writer (1834–1867)
WARE, EUGENE FITCH (Ironquill), lawyer-poet (1841–1911)
WASHINGTON, GEORGE, President (1732–1799)
WATTERSON, HENRY, editor (1840–1921)
WEBSTER, DANIEL, senator (1782–1852)
WELLER, CHARLES E., typing teacher (1840–1925)
WHARTON, EDITH (JONES), novelist (1862–1937)
WHITE, E. B. (ELWYN BROOKS), author (1899–   )
WHITE, WILLIAM ALLEN, editor (1868–1944)
WHITMAN, WALT, poet (1819–1892)
WHITTIER, JOHN GREENLEAF, poet (1807–1892)
WILCOX, ELLA WHEELER, poet (1855–1919)
WILLIS, NATHANIEL PARKER, editor (1806–1867)
WILLKIE, WENDELL L., political leader (1892–1944)
WILSON, WOODROW, President (1856–1924)
WINTHROP, JOHN, Pilgrim (1588–1649)
WISTER, OWEN, author (1860–1938)
WOODWORTH, SAMUEL, writer (1784–1842)
WOOLLCOTT, ALEXANDER, critic (1887–1943)
WORK, HENRY CLAY, poet (1832–1884)

THE EDITOR AND HIS BOOK

CHARLES HURD, *author, journalist and public relations consultant, was born May 11, 1903, in Tonkawa, Oklahoma. He received his boyhood education from tutors; from 1918 to 1923 he was an extension student at Northwestern University, Evanston, Illinois. During his college years, Hurd became a full-time reporter for the Associated Press in Chicago, and later, in New York City. In 1926 he became an associate editor of* Liberty *Magazine. Three years later he left* Liberty *to join the staff of the New York* Times, *Washington, D.C. Bureau and remained there (except for a two-year stint as London Correspondent) until 1949. Six of these years were spent as a White House Correspondent.*

Since 1949 he has been actively engaged as a writer and as an industrial public relations counselor with his own firm, Charles Hurd & Associates.

Through the years Mr. Hurd has contributed articles to leading national magazines including Life, Redbook *and* Reader's Digest. *His published books are:* The White House (*Harper, 1940*); The Veterans Program (*Whittlesey House, 1945*); Calvacade of America (*Dutton, 1947*); The Compact History of the American Red Cross (*Hawthorn, 1959*); A Treasury of Great American Speeches (*Hawthorn, 1959*); U.S. Mail, *in collaboration with Arthur E. Summerfield* (*Holt, 1960*); Calvalcade of Europe, *in collaboration with Lowell Thomas* (*Doubleday, 1960*); A Treasury of Great American Letters (*Hawthorn, 1961*).

A HAWTHORN BOOK

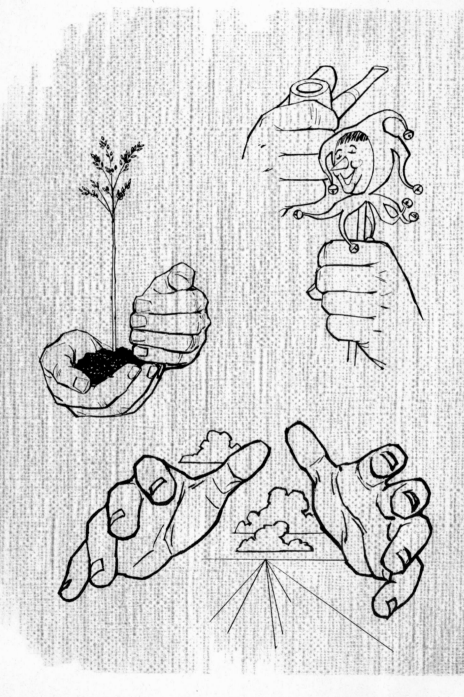